THE QUIET TIME NOTEBOOK

ALSO BY CATHERINE MARTIN

⸻

Six Secrets to a Powerful Quiet Time
Knowing and Loving the Bible
Walking with the God Who Cares
Set my Heart on Fire
Trusting in the Names of God
Passionate Prayer
A Heart That Hopes in God
Run Before the Wind
Trusting in the Names of God—A Quiet Time Experience
Passionate Prayer—A Quiet Time Experience
Pilgrimage of the Heart
Revive My Heart
A Heart That Dances
A Heart on Fire
A Heart to See Forever
Quiet Time Moments for Women
Drawing Strength from the Names of God
A Woman's Heart that Dances
A Woman's Walk in Grace
The Quiet Time Journal
The Devotional Bible Study Notebook
The Passionate Prayer Notebook

⸻

CATHERINE MARTIN

THE QUIET TIME NOTEBOOK

Quiet Time
M I N I S T R I E S

PALM DESERT, CALIFORNIA

Cover by Quiet Time Ministries.
Cover photo by Catherine Martin—myPhotoWalk.com

The Quiet Time Notebook
Copyright © 1994—2013 by Catherine Martin
Published by Quiet Time Ministries
Palm Desert, California 92255
www.quiettime.org

ISBN-13: 978-0-9766886-2-4

Second Edition published by Quiet Time Ministries 2013

Printed in the United States of America
13 14 15 16 17 18 19 20 21 / ACS /11 10 9 8 7 6 5 4 3 2

EX LIBRIS

❊

Dates

❊

My Key Word & Verse

❊

One thing I have asked from the LORD, that I shall seek:
that I may dwell in the house of the LORD all the days of my life,
to behold the beauty of the LORD and to meditate in His temple.

PSALM 27:4 NASB

——❈——

Thus says the LORD, "Let not a wise man boast of his wisdom,
and let not the mighty man boast of his might,
let not a rich man boast of his riches; but let him who boasts boast of this,
that he understands and knows Me, that I am the LORD who exercises lovingkindness,
justice and righteousness on earth; for I delight in these things," declares the LORD.

JEREMIAH 9:23-24 NASB

——❈——

At the heart of your relationship with the Lord is time with Him—quiet time. Quiet
time with God every day is initiated by God, led by God, and enriched by God. He has
provided everything necessary for intimacy: the Word of God, the indwelling Holy Spirit,
the companionship of Jesus, and the fellowship of good friends…God is extending an
invitation to you to be intimate with Him. To know Him. To walk with Him.
It is an invitation to radical intimacy.

CATHERINE MARTIN, SIX SECRETS TO A POWERFUL QUIET TIME

——❈——

∽ CONTENTS ∽

꧁ INTRODUCTION ꧂

Your life is a journey. You are the beloved of God. You were created to know and love God. The great fulfillment in life for you is intimacy with God. God extends an invitation to you to embrace Him by receiving forgiveness of sins through the payment of sin's penalty by His Beloved Son, Jesus Christ. This is good news because now you may experience forever your true purpose in life and all that you were created for—intimacy with God. Jesus has made it possible. At some point in your life you must answer the invitation of God and embrace Him through Jesus Christ. Pray a simple prayer: *Lord Jesus, I need You. Thank You for dying on the cross for my sins. I invite you now to come into my life, forgive my sins, and make me the person You want me to be.* When you pray that prayer and surrender your life to Jesus, your life moves from simply a journey to an adventure. Corrie Ten Boom calls our life of faith a "Fantastic Adventure In Trusting Him."

The wonderful truth is that the more you know of God, the more you can know Him. The intimacy you begin to enjoy with the Lord may increase. There is a major requirement to enjoy growth in your knowledge of God and intimacy with Him—much time spent alone with the Lord. All the men and women of God in the past who have experienced intimacy with the Lord have learned the discipline of time alone with God.

I remember early on sitting in a room with a group of students. We had all recently committed our lives to the Lord Jesus Christ. We were listening to a speaker talk about our relationship with Jesus and what it truly means to be committed to Christ. I can just imagine how he felt, looking into our faces, almost seeing into our hearts, filled with passion and excitement. We had not yet begun to fight the fight of faith or persevere through storms in life. And so, in the middle of his message, he stopped. He spoke directly with great seriousness. "You know, in ten years, only a very small percentage of you will be walking closely with the Lord." Well, that room got very silent. We were stunned. We looked at each other. I think we all felt as though we were the twelve disciples, hearing Jesus say, "One of you will betray me." We thought, "No way!" But, guess what. Ten years later, only a very small percentage of us were walking closely with the Lord. What can encourage a lifelong experience of intimacy with God and faithfulness to Him through years of victory, triumph, difficulties and adversity? I believe the one great thing that will make a difference is much time spent alone with God in His Word.

This time alone with God is known as your quiet time. It is the most important time you will spend each day. The time and effort you invest in your relationship with the Lord now will determine the intimacy you enjoy with Him in the future.

In ministry over the years, both on staff with Campus Crusade for Christ, leading Bible studies, and in seminary, I have been approached numerous times for help in how to have a quiet time

---

with the Lord. The almost universal question has been, "Where do I begin?" It is an awesome prospect to think about spending time alone with the Almighty God, the Creator of the universe, the King of Kings, and the Lord of Lords.

I am a traveller just like you in this journey of life. I have joined in the great adventure of living each day to the hilt in an intimate relationship with God. Contained within these pages is something of my own passion and pursuit of God. It is a sharing of ideas and a guide into quiet time with the Lord. For years I have chronicled my adventure with the Lord in a notebook. This notebook has taken many forms and has developed as I have grown and learned new ways to enhance my time with Him in both prayer and study of God's Word.

In *The Quiet Time Notebook*, I will help you get started in your quiet time with the Lord. To learn more about how to have a quiet time and to use your Quiet Time Notebook, I encourage you to read the 30-Day Journey I've written entitled *Six Secrets To A Powerful Quiet Time*. Then, to learn how to incorporate devotional Bible study into your quiet time, I encourage you to read the 30-Day Journey I've written entitled *Knowing And Loving The Bible* and get *The Devotional Bible Study Notebook*. To grow in your life of prayer, I encourage you to read the 30-Day Journey of *Passionate Prayer—Discover the Power of Talking With God* and add *The Passionate Prayer Notebook* to your quiet time resources. Walking with the Lord and growing in your relationship begins in your quiet time where you will draw near to Him, open the pages of your Bible, hear Him speak in His Word, and commune with Him in prayer, worship and adoration.

You hold in your hands some of the fruit of what God has been teaching me about quiet time over the course of many years, *The Quiet Time Notebook*. Over the years, I've used *The Quiet Time Notebook* pages, drawing me deeper into intimacy with God, and teaching me more and more how to walk by faith in His Word. I look at all of life as the great adventure of knowing God. Through intention and purpose and planning, we can grow more intimate with the Lord, sharing His heart all along the way.

Our first question should always be, no matter what we face in life, "What is God's heart in this? What is He doing? What does He have in mind?" Our quiet time with God will help us seek God first in everything. David, the man after God's own heart, expressed his one great desire in Psalm 27:4. "One thing I have asked from the LORD, that I shall seek; that I may dwell in the house of the LORD all the days of my life, to behold the beauty of the LORD and to meditate in His temple." That verse became my life verse many years ago. And out of my desire to experience all that is in that verse, God gave me the idea to put together *The Quiet Time Notebook*, first for myself, and then, years later, for you.

The *Quiet Time Notebook* contains pages for your quiet time. These pages include:

- Prepare Your Heart Journal pages

- Read and Study God's Word pages

- Adore God in Prayer pages

- Yield, Enjoy, Rest pages

- Reference Study pages

- Notes pages

These pages can be used in many ways as you spend time with the Lord in your quiet time. The Prepare Your Heart Journal pages are your journal and offer a place write out your thoughts and insights from your time alone with God in His Word. In the Read and Study God's Word pages, you will discover a place to write insights as you dig deeper in God's Word. The Adore God in Prayer pages will give you a place for your prayers and answers to prayers. The Yield, Enjoy, Rest pages will help you apply God's Word to your life. And then, the Reference Study pages will give you a place to write out insights from different verses in the Bible based on one theme or topic. The Notes pages offer a place for your to record sermon and message notes. The sky is the limit to how many ways you can use this notebook in your own quiet time. I encourage you to ask the Lord to lead and guide you as you draw near to Him using *The Quiet Time Notebook*.

I will help get you started in The Quiet Time Notebook Guide chapters. Those chapters include The P.R.A.Y.E.R. Quiet Time Plan, ways to enrich your quiet time, detailed instructions and examples for each page of *The Quiet Time Notebook*, Bible Reading Plans, a Quiet Time Worksheet, and Monthly Quiet Time Reflection pages.

The Quiet Time Notebook is designed to be a resource for you in your quiet time. It's a place for you to write things that the Lord teaches you as you draw near to Him. And when its pages are filled, you will have a testimony in written form of your intimate relationship with God. You will notice there is a place at the front of *The Quiet Time Notebook* for you to write your name, the dates, and a key verse. You may use more than one *Quiet Time Notebook* in a year, and these notebooks will be chronicles of your adventure with the Lord as you grow in your knowledge of Him.

Would you like to become consistent in spending time alone with the Lord? Would you like to learn new ways to enhance your quiet time? Would you like to know God more and grow in your relationship with Him? *The Quiet Time Notebook*, offering variety, flexibility, and the opportunity for spontaneity in your relationship with the Lord, is designed to enrich your quiet time. My prayer is that you will come with an open, teachable heart, hungry for God. Personalize this notebook, experimenting and exploring its possibilities in your own relationship with the Lord.

Reading a concept is no substitute for the hands-on excitement of the pursuit of God. I would not have you simply watch a travelogue on the Holy Land. I would rather you touch for yourself the blades of grass on the Mount of Olives and watch the sun glisten on the Sea of Galilee. My prayer is that you will "taste and see that the Lord is good" (Psalm 34:8 NASB).

So dear friend, will you set aside the many things for the one thing in life, the great pursuit of knowing God? Someday you will stand face to face with your Lord. I want you to be able to look into eyes that are familiar to you because you have spent much time with Him now. I want you to enjoy His beauty and experience His love. When you are face to face with Him, you will know that your time alone with Him in prayer was worth it all. God bless you, dear friend, as you engage in the great adventure of knowing Him.

QUIET TIME MINISTRIES ONLINE

Quiet Time Ministries Online at www.quiettime.org is a place where you can deepen your devotion to God and His Word. Cath's Blog is where Catherine shares about life, about the Lord, and just about everything else. A Walk In Grace™ is Catherine's devotional photojournal, highlighting her own photography, where you can grow deep in the garden of His grace. Quiet Time Ministries proudly sponsors Ministry For Women at www.ministryforwomen.com—a social network community for women worldwide to grow in their relationship with Jesus Christ. Connect, study, and grow at Ministry For Women. Quiet Time Ministries proudly sponsors Catherine Martin's myPhotoWalk at www.myphotowalk.com where lovers of photography can experience the great adventure of knowing God through Devotional Photography.

MY LETTER TO THE LORD

As you begin using *The Quiet Time Notebook*, I'd like to ask, where are you? What has been happening in your life over the last year or so? What has been your life experience? What are you facing and what has God been teaching you? It is no accident that you have *The Quiet Time Notebook* to use in your quiet time. In fact, God has something He wants you to know, something that will change the whole landscape of your experience with Him. Watch for it, listen for it, and when you learn it, write it down and never let it go. Will you write a prayer in the form of a letter to the Lord in the space provided expressing all that is on your heart and ask Him to speak to you as you draw near and grow in the great adventure of knowing Him?

MY LETTER TO THE LORD

THE QUIET TIME NOTEBOOK GUIDE

THE P.R.A.Y.E.R. QUIET TIME PLAN

But Jesus Himself would often slip away to the wilderness to pray.
LUKE 5:16

Quiet time with your Lord is an incredible privilege. It's a gift of grace given by your Lord. So where do you begin? This is a question we've all thought about at different times on our journey with the Lord. I like to keep it simple and these are the main things I return to time and time again. Begin with a time, a place, and a plan. Jesus set the example for us in quiet time.

> "In the early morning, while it was still dark, Jesus got up, left the house, and went away to a secluded place, and was prying there" (Mark 1:35).
> "But Jesus Himself would often slip away to the wilderness and pray" (Luke 5:16).

As you can see, the Lord Jesus was intentional about His time with the Father. He had specific times, went to specific places, and did specific things in His quiet time. The time, the place and the plan sets the stage for all the magnificent things that happen in time alone with the Lord.

THE QUIET TIME

One of the first things that I learned in developing a quiet time with the Lord was that it involved intentional devotion. Quiet time is not something that just happens. It requires planning and preparation. If the president of the United States called you and invited you to lunch, you would not say, "Maybe I will, maybe I won't." You would say, "What time and where?" Think about it this way. The Lord, who is the CEO of the universe, desires time with you each day. We cannot say, "Maybe I will and maybe I won't." The response is, "What time and where?" Ask the Lord to help you determine the time. After all, God created you for fellowship with Him. He will make a way. Remember, the goal is *radical intimacy* with the Lord. Radical intimacy implies *radical choices* for the Lord against many good things that would keep us from being alone with Him. God will honor the sacrifice in time, energy, and sometimes even sleep to be alone with Him.

When is the best time to spend with the Lord? The Bible seems to emphasize the importance of the morning (Mark 1:35). David said in Psalm 5:3, "In the morning, O LORD, You will hear my voice; In the morning I will order my prayer to You and eagerly watch." In the morning Jacob made a vow to the Lord and set up a stone on the ground as a memorial to the Lord (Genesis 28:18). Moses made one of the grandest prayer requests when he said, "Lord, show me your glory…" (Exodus 33:18). God answered Moses' request in the morning when "The Lord descended in the cloud and stood there with him as he called upon the name of the LORD" (Exodus 34:5). Probably the greatest encouragement of all for quiet time in the morning is seen in the life of Jesus Himself. "In the early morning, while it was still dark, Jesus got up, left the house, and went away to a secluded place, and was praying there" (Mark 1:35).

The time you choose should be when you are most alert and you can be completely alone with the Lord. Sometimes, quiet time in the morning is absolutely impossible. For you, it may be midday or at night. Quiet time is a time when you withdraw from the activities and distractions of the world to sit alone with the Lord in His Word and in prayer.

Finding a time with the Lord will involve creativity and resourcefulness. It will also mean a certain ruthlessness that says no to other things in order to say yes to the Lord. You are going to learn the art of "slipping away" that Jesus practiced during His stay on earth (Luke 5:15-16). M. Basil Pennington says in his book, *A Place Apart*, "What person can dare say they cannot afford to take time for apartness—indeed, who can afford not to take time for apartness?…There is in the lives of most of us a good bit more freedom and flexibility to organize such a dimension, *if we really want to*."[1] Ask the Lord to show you the best time.

I remember one young mother who was so excited about beginning to spend time with the Lord. She got up early, brewed her coffee, and gathered her quiet time materials. Then, she sat down to have quiet time with the Lord. Within minutes, she heard the footsteps of her young children coming down the hall to join her. Did she give up? No. This creative mother decided to help her young children establish their own quiet times. She explained that she was having quiet time with the Lord. She helped them each sit down and be alone with the Lord. Soon, those little ones could not wait to get up early and have a quiet time just like their mother. Another lady came up to me and said there was absolutely not one moment in the day that she could spend time with the Lord. I suggested she ask the Lord to find a time for her. Later, she came up to me and excitedly shared how God had shown her that she could draw near to Him during her lunch hour.

People often ask me how much time I spend with the Lord. My answer is: sometimes ten minutes and sometimes two hours. It all depends how much time I have and how much time I am willing to set aside to know the Lord. My quiet time is usually about an hour. But sometimes, the Lord takes me on a journey in His Word, and then I tarry even longer with Him. Like all relationships of friendship and intimacy, our times together vary in length and intensity. But if we miss these bonding moments or rush too many of our times together, we miss a richness and depth of love. Connecting on an intimate level is the goal. A.W. Tozer wrote in his first editorial for *Alliance Weekly* dated June 3, 1950, "It will cost something to walk slow in the parade of the ages while excited men of time rush about confusing motion with progress. But it will pay in the long run and the true Christian is not much interested in anything short of that."

THE QUIET PLACE

Radical intimacy flourishes in a quiet place. God says, "In quietness and trust is your strength" (Isaiah 30:15). Have you found your quiet "place" with the Lord?

It is clear that Jesus was the master of the art of finding the quiet place (Luke 5:15-16). When He wanted to commune with His Father and spend time with intimate friends, He would travel to Bethany, two miles from Jerusalem on the far side of the Mount of Olives, out in the country, covered with fruit trees and waving grain. Jesus probably walked to Bethany after busy days in Jerusalem, savoring the journey with His Father. His friends often observed Him amid the trees or the grassy fields, in deep communion with God the Father.

Everyone needs a Bethany. Jesus invites you to "Come with Me by yourselves to a quiet place and rest a little while" (Mark 6:31 WMS). Henri Nouwen says that "we have, indeed, to fashion our own desert where we can withdraw every day, shake off our compulsions, and dwell in the gentle healing presence of our Lord."[2]

Robert Murray McCheyne, a pastor at St. Peter's Church in Dundee, Scotland, in the early 1800s embarked on a rigorous ministry trip through Europe. McCheyne and his fellow travelers encountered a raging storm on the Mediterranean Sea and were forced to land on a desert island. Listen to what McCheyne said about this event in the letter to his church contained in the *Memoirs and Remains of Robert Murray McCheyne* by Andrew Bonar:

> I thought that perhaps this providence was given me that I might have a quiet day to pray for you. There were about twelve fishermen's huts on the island, made of reeds, with a vine growing before the door, and a fig tree in their garden. We gave tracts and books in French to all our fellow passengers, and to the inhabitants, and tried to hallow the Sabbath. My heart went up to God the whole day for you all, and for my dear friends who would be ministering to you. I tried to go over you one by one, as many as I could call to mind. My longing desire for you was, that Jesus might reveal Himself to you in the breaking of bread, that you might have heart–filling views of the lovely person of Immanuel, and might draw from Him rivers of comfort, life, and holiness.[3]

That remote island became a sanctuary for McCheyne. With God there, it was holy ground— McCheyne's quiet place.

When do you need this quiet place? Everyday, especially in challenging life situations. You need to "come away" *when you get troubling news.* When Jesus heard the news about the death of John the Baptist, He left in a boat to find a quiet place alone (Matthew 14:13). Then, you need a quiet place *in a time of popularity and success.* One time a whole city gathered at the door where Jesus was staying. What did Jesus do? He got up early in the morning and went to a deserted place and prayed there (Mark 1:35). You need a quiet place *after a time of intense ministry.* After the disciples came back from their ministry adventure of preaching and teaching that the Lord invited them to come away with Him and rest awhile (Mark 6:31-32). Finally, you need a quiet place *when there are huge demands on you and you have little time to yourself.* Jesus was constantly surrounded by people. What would He do? He would leave the place where He was staying and find a quiet place (Luke 5:15-16).

A.W. Tozer, pastor of Chicago's Southside Alliance church and Editor of *Alliance Weekly*, was a man who enjoyed great popularity in his ministry and yet he was known as one who spent much time in his office, with his door closed, alone with God. One biographer noted that Tozer spent more time on his knees than at his desk. Another person noted that "this man makes you want to know and feel God." Tozer simply was not ruled by the success that adorned his life. He walked with God. His tombstone bears the simple epitaph: A Man Of God. The secret: making the quiet place a priority.

THE QUIET TIME PLAN

Intimacy becomes radical when you become intentional with God—with a revolutionary plan to draw near to Him. Paul was very intentional: "I count all things to be loss in view of the surpassing value of knowing Christ Jesus my Lord, for whom I have suffered the loss of all things, and count them but rubbish so that I may gain Christ" (Philippians 3:8). Over the years, I have discovered there are certain disciplines of devotion found in the Bible that help me become a participant, experiencing the character and person of the Lord in my own life. Henri Nouwen defines discipline as "the effort to create some space in which God can act."[4] Biblical devotional disciplines include such things as prayer, Bible study, meditating on God's Word, solitude, devotional reading, journaling, listening to God, submission to God, worship, and practical application. A quiet time plan embraces different devotional disciplines to draw you into God's Word, hear Him speak, and respond to Him in prayer.

In Mark 9:29, Jesus makes a very important statement about prayer and quiet time in the context of the healing of a demon-possessed boy. Jesus admonishes His disciples, "This kind [of demon] cannot come out by anything but prayer." But when did Jesus pray? Luke 9:28 gives us the answer. It says that "[Jesus] took along Peter and John and James and went up to the mountain to pray…while He was praying the appearance of His face became different and His clothing became white and gleaming." This event occurred just prior to the healing of the boy. When He speaks about prayer in this passage He is not referring to a single request offered to God, but an entire lifestyle, a habit of life. He is talking about quiet time. *Prayer is first and foremost an ongoing, dynamic, intimate relationship with God that must be tended, nurtured, and cultivated through specific times of communion and fellowship with Him*…quiet time. That is why the word *PRAYER* is such a good way to remember how to spend time alone with the Lord.

THE P.R.A.Y.E.R. QUIET TIME PLAN

Prepare Your Heart

Read and Study God's Word

Adore God in Prayer

Yield Yourself to God

Enjoy His Presence

Rest in His Love

- *Prepare Your Heart*—James 4:8 encourages you to "draw near to God and He will draw near to you." Prepare Your Heart includes simple prayer, solitude, silence, journaling, and spiritual meditation.

- *Read And Study God's Word*—In Colossians 3:16, Paul encourages you to "let the word of Christ richly dwell within you." Read and Study God's Word includes a Bible reading plan, observation, interpretation, and application.

- *Adore God In Prayer*—In 1 Thessalonians 5:17, Paul says to "pray without ceasing." Adore God In Prayer includes adoration, confession, thanksgiving, supplication, writing prayer requests, praying for the world, and praying Scripture.

- *Yield Yourself To God*—In 1 Peter 5:6, Peter says, "Humble yourselves under the mighty hand of God, that He may exalt you at the proper time." Yield Yourself To God includes humility, submission, brokenness, and surrender to God.

- *Enjoy His Presence*—The psalmist says, "Delight yourself in the Lord, and He will give you the desires of your heart" (Psalm 37:4). Enjoy His Presence includes practicing the presence of God as well as moment by moment prayer, extended times with the Lord, and personal retreats.

- *Rest in His Love*—Jesus said, "Come to Me, all who are weary and heavy-laden, and I will give you rest" (Matthew 11:28). Rest in His Love through sharing the life of Christ, discipleship, knowing the heart of Jesus, and bringing every part of your life to Him.

Once you learn the devotional disciplines of this quiet time plan, you will want to personalize it as the Lord leads you in your adventure with Him. This plan is flexible and may be used as a guideline whether you have ten minutes or two hours to spend with the Lord. It is a tool that is learned, practiced, and developed over a lifetime. With the time, the place, and the plan, quiet time is no longer a seemingly unattainable mystery, but an exciting adventure. Quiet time is not an end in itself, but a means to your desired goal: radical intimacy—the great adventure of knowing God.

OVERVIEW OF YOUR QUIET TIME NOTEBOOK

Be still and know that I am God.
Psalm 46:10

I n your quiet time it is important to write down what you have learned—for memory, for meditation, and for comprehension. When I began spending time with God, I used a spiral notebook as a journal. Then, I got another notebook to keep track of my prayer requests and answers to prayer. As I began studying God's Word, I used another notebook to write out all that God was teaching me from His Word. I'll never forget the day in my quiet time when the Lord gave me the idea to get a notebook with dividers, and combine all those notebooks into one notebook. For years I used that notebook in my quiet time and found that it helped me stay consistent and intentional in my time alone with the Lord. Then one morning in my quiet time, the Lord turned my thoughts to you. Of course, I may not know your name, but I was thinking about my precious brothers and sisters in the Lord who wanted to grow deeper and more intimate in their relationship with the Lord. "Lord," I prayed, "I long to encourage others to know You more and love You with all their hearts." A big idea came to my mind. Why not put together a Quiet Time Notebook just like what I use in my own quiet time. That notebook has been available through Quiet Time Ministries for almost twenty years. You hold in your hands the result of that prayer so many years ago. *The Quiet Time Notebook* is a resource that will help you draw near to God in His Word and in prayer through quiet time. What is the great result? You will experience the great adventure of knowing God.

OVERVIEW OF THE QUIET TIME NOTEBOOK

There are six sections in your notebook. The first four sections correspond to P.R.A.Y.E.R.™ Quiet Time Plan™ (Prepare Your Heart, Read And Study God's Word, Adore God In Prayer, Yield Yourself To God, Enjoy His Presence and Rest In His Love). This plan is designed to help you remember all you can do in your quiet time. Please note: you may not necessarily use all these notebook sections at once during your quiet time. In fact, at times you may use only the Prepare

Journal pages or the Adore God prayer pages. On some days you may use another section of the notebook. These pages are designed to enrich your quiet time. The fifth section, Reference Study, may be used for more in-depth inductive Bible Study. The final section, Notes, provides a place to record insights from sermons, commentaries, books, and audio/video messages.

First, I want to begin with an overview of all the sections for those of you who want a quick read, and long to just dive in and use the notebook pages in your quiet time. You may also use the overview for quick reference and refreshment. Following this overview, I will include detailed instruction and examples for each page. I encourage you to study and experiment with these pages in your quiet time.

PREPARE YOUR HEART JOURNAL PAGES

This initial element of your daily quiet time sets the tone for all that follows. It is the preparation of your heart to meet with the Lord. Your goal is to quiet your heart, asking God to open your spiritual eyes and ears, and give you a teachable heart. When you draw near to God, He promises to draw near to you (James 4:8). As you begin your time with God, there are many different ways to quiet your heart and draw near to God. You may meditate on a Psalm or Proverb, reflect on a devotional reading from a daily devotional or favorite book, or worship the Lord in song using a hymnbook or favorite praise music. Write your initial thoughts, reflections, prayers and insights in your Journal found in the first section of your notebook.

READ AND STUDY GOD'S WORD PAGES

God desires to teach you about His character, His ways, His desires, and His dreams for you as the person you are meant to be. He accomplishes this through His Word, the Bible. The words in the Bible are the outward expression of God's thoughts and feelings in a language you may understand. His ultimate goal is that you become involved with Him, know Him firsthand, and grow in an intimate love relationship with Him, becoming more and more like Christ. It is imperative that you spend time living in a portion of God's Word each day. Choose a Bible reading plan (a number of options are included in a later chapter). The Read and Study pages are designed to incorporate simple devotional Bible study methods enabling you to glean biblical truth from your daily time in God's Word. Use the Read and Study pages on those days when you desire to dig deeper into God's Word and you have extra time. As you incorporate devotional Bible study into your quiet time, biblical truth will become more clear and you will more easily apply it to your life. If you are in another ongoing Bible Study, you will use that study in place of using this section of your notebook. However, sometimes you may want to use one of these pages to explore a significant verse even from an ongoing Bible study. The Read and Study pages include

One Significant Observation, Immediate Context, Insights/Word Meanings, Cross-References, Summary and Conclusions, and Application in My Life.

ADORE GOD IN PRAYER PAGES

Prayer is the lifting up of one's soul to God. God will teach you to pray as you learn about His character, ways, and desires through study of His Word. As you begin this special time of conversing and communing with God, the acrostic ACTS will help you remember ways to pray. Adore God by meditating on what you have learned about Him and His ways. You might spend some time in silence before Him, contemplating His majesty and glory. Then, Confess sins that come to your mind. By faith, Thank Him for His forgiveness and cleansing by the blood of Jesus Christ. Remember God's blessings and review all God has done on your behalf. Finally, make Supplications (your requests) known to God as you draw near to His throne of grace. The Adore God In Prayer pages offer space to write out your requests to God, verses God brings to your mind in relation to your requests, and God's answers to prayer. Writing out your requests gives you the opportunity to see the amazing ways that God answers your prayers and works in your life.

YIELD, ENJOY, REST PAGES

These final elements of your daily quiet time plan allows for a brief time of reflection, application, and preparation to go out into the world and live out what God has made known to you in private. Yield Yourself To God, and place any unfulfilled dreams and desires in the hands of the Lord. Humble yourself before the Lord and remain open to His plans, asking Him to teach you His ways and eternal perspective. Use the space provided to write a brief prayer expressing what is on your heart. To Enjoy His Presence, place today's responsibilities, activities, and appointments in the hands of the Lord. Record any special prayer requests related to your day. Write one significant truth you have learned from the Lord to think about throughout the day. As you leave this quiet time and place of prayer, the Lord goes with you. Talk to Him unceasingly, and share every experience of life with Him. He loves you. Then, Rest In His Love. As you bask in the vast ocean of God's love, you will experience the surpassing riches of His grace and kindness. Place any anxious thoughts, conflicts, or difficult circumstances in the hands of the Lord. You may want to record a promise from God's Word related to your need. Your goal is to remain in His love. The result is rest and refreshment, producing within you a life glorifying to God.

REFERENCE STUDY PAGES

A reference study may be accomplished separately or in conjunction with your daily time in God's Word. It is your opportunity to explore other verses in the Bible related to a verse, phrase, word, or topic. The Reference Study pages with space available to record each verse and any insights. Try to include a Reference Study in your Quiet Time at least once a week or even once a month.

NOTES PAGES

As you study various passages of Scripture, you will want to do further reading and study to enhance your study, choosing from among books, commentaries, magazine articles. The Notes Section is a convenient place to record what you learn from your studies as you listen to lectures, sermons, audio or video, or read books, articles, or commentaries.

PUTTING IT ALL TOGETHER

I encourage you to experiment with these notebook pages. Certain pages and sections will become your favorites. In the next chapter, I will give you detailed instructions and examples of each page. Then, following that chapter you will find ways to enrich your quiet time and even a worksheet to begin and plan for your quiet time. I hope you're getting excited. The Lord will lead you into a deep and rich time with Him.

HOW TO USE YOUR QUIET TIME NOTEBOOK

So let us know, let us press on to know the LORD.
HOSEA 6:3

Quiet time is the grand experiment. You can do something new in your quiet time every day and never exhaust the possibilities of devotion to God. Hosea said, "So let us know, let us press on to know the LORD. His going forth is as certain as the dawn; and He will come to us like the rain, like the spring rain watering the earth" (Hosea 6:3). Pressing on to know the Lord means that you will be intentional and persistent in pursuing God, day by day, and moment by moment. You will discover that *The Quiet Time Notebook* is going to be your friend and companion in helping you focus on knowing the Lord. The world will encourage you to remain shallow, assume a spectator position, and spend little time alone with God. The Lord Jesus, through His Spirit, will encourage exactly the opposite. He longs for intimacy. He invites you to abide in Him (John 15:4). The NIV translation uses the word "remain," encouraging you to stay close, and never leave your Lord or step away from intimacy with Him. He says, "Come to Me, all you who are weary and heavy laden, and I will give you rest" (Matthew 28:18). Your Quiet Time Notebook is the place for you to keep a living testimony of your communion and companionship with your Lord.

In the pages that follow, you will discover instructions and examples for each of the notebook pages. I am including such detail so that you will know how to use a page when you are ready to include it in your quiet time. However, please know that these pages are meant to be used as a tool in your quiet time, and they won't all be used together in one sitting. Sometimes, the tendency at first is to think that you must use each page every day. That's not the normal use of *The Quiet Time Notebook*. As I mentioned before, sometimes you may only use one or two pages like the Prepare Your Heart Journal page or Adore God in Prayer page. In Chapter 4 I will share different ways to use the pages in your quiet time. For now, read through these instructions, look at the examples, and begin the great adventure of knowing God more in your quiet time.

PREPARE YOUR HEART JOURNAL

Tools You Will Need: Cross-Reference Bible, *The Quiet Time Notebook*
Optional Tools: Daily Devotionals, Devotional Reading, Hymnbook, Praise and
Worship Music

The initial element of your daily quiet time sets the tone for all that follows. As you prepare to meet with the Lord, quiet your heart, asking God to open your spiritual eyes and ears, speak to you, and give you a teachable spirit. The following are ways to Prepare Your Heart:

- Pray, asking God to prepare you to meet alone with Him.

- Spend time in silence before God.

- Write initial thoughts and reflections using the Prepare Your Heart Journal page.

- Meditate on a Psalm or Proverb from the Psalms and Proverbs reading plan (in Chapter 6). Write insights in the Prepare Your Heart Journal.

- Reflect upon a devotional reading from a devotional book or daily devotional. I highly recommend *My Utmost For His Highest* by Oswald Chambers, *Morning and Evening* by Charles Haddon Spurgeon, or *Daily Light.*

- Sing to the Lord using your hymnbook or listen to songs of praise and worship.

Prepare Your Heart Journal pages are the place to express your deep thoughts, contemplative moments, and heart meditations of God. In it you will chronicle your adventure with God. As you read what you have written through the years, you will be in awe as you see the hand of God at work in your life.

1. *Contemplation*: As you read from devotional books, read and study God's Word, or pray, take time along the way to contemplate great truths, listening to the Lord in the quiet moments.

2. *Expression*: Alternate between listening to God and meditation upon the truth of God's Word (or profound thoughts in devotional books), then express what you see and learn about God and yourself by writing out your thoughts and prayers. You might ask, "Where am I?" Write your answer in your journal, evaluating your spiritual, physical, and emotional life and circumstances. Your writing on your Prepare Your Heart Journal pages may include Scripture, your insights about the beauty of God's creation, daily blessings, your present situation your feelings about your circumstances, God's perspective, what God is teaching you, your dreams, desires, goals, insights and responses to what you have read, ministry ideas, lecture outlines, prayers and psalms, poetry, stories, quotes, art, pencil sketches, and photography.

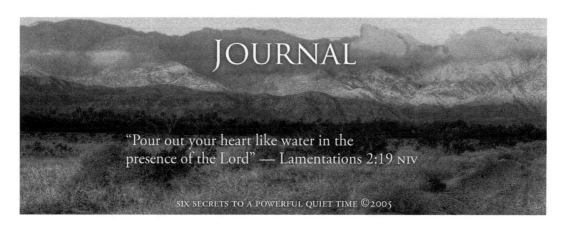

"Pour out your heart like water in the
presence of the Lord" — Lamentations 2:19 NIV

SIX SECRETS TO A POWERFUL QUIET TIME ©2005

January 21, 2005 I love what John Henry Jowett says today in "The
Things Which Lead To Peace." He says there is a great reward for
meditation and obedience. "The God of Peace shall be with you."
He goes on to say, "And that is everything. If the king is present at
the table, a crust is a feast. If the Lord is on the battlefield, then
amid all the surrounding turbulence there is a centre of peace. When
the God of peace is in the life, there is a chamber in which the sound
of warfare never comes." I have truly experienced that what Jowett
says is true. My relationship with the Lord is that one thing no one
and nothing can touch.

READ AND STUDY GOD'S WORD

Tools You Will Need: Cross-Reference Bible, *The Quiet Time Notebook,* Exhaustive Concordance, *NASB Hebrew-Greek Key Word Study Bible.*

1. *Date – Today's Scripture*: Record today's date and Scripture reference on the Read and Study page. If you are involved in an ongoing group Bible Study, you may complete that study prior to or in place of using this section of your notebook.

2. *Read God's Word*: Read today's Scripture from your chosen Bible reading plan.

3. *Record One Significant Observation*: As you carefully read God's Word, record your Most Significant Observation. This will be the word, phrase, verse, or insight that impressed you the most.

4. *Immediate Context*: Take into consideration surrounding verses and life situation to put yourself into the environment of the passage. Using your imagination, identify with the characters and situations found in your chosen passage. How does your significant observation relate to the entire chapter in which you found it? Summarize the main event, subject, or idea in passage in one sentence. For more information on context, you may wish to consult the NIV or NASB Study Bible or a one volume commentary.

5. *Insight – Word Meanings – Cross References*: Think about your significant observation. To explore its meaning, you may complete Insights, Word Meanings, and/or Cross-References. Insights are meaningful observations or ideas that come to your mind as you live in God's Word. You may choose to simply write your thoughts about your observation. Then, you may do a simple devotional study by defining one word or looking up one cross-reference. More details are presented on next page.

5. *Summary & Conclusions*: In 2 or 3 sentences, summarize what you have learned from your study, keeping in mind immediate context.

6. *Application in My Life*: Record 1 or 2 sentences on how what you have learned applies to your life, reviewing and responding to at least one of the following questions: How does what you have learned give you God's view of your present situation in life? What do you learn about God and His ways? Is there something God wants you to obey? Have you been convicted of sin, requiring confession and repentance? Is there a verse to memorize? How has God met your needs and present circumstances in life today? Is there a prayer on your heart compelling you to pour out your heart to God? Is there an example from which you can pattern your life? Do you see a doctrinal or ethical truth? Is there anything that affects your goals in life, giving you new meaning and purpose? Did you discover a letter or email you need to write? Do you have a person in your life you need to love and encourage?

There are many ways for you to traverse the landscape of God's Word in devotional Bible study as you dig deeper in Scripture, hearing the Lord speak, teaching you about your significant observation. The Read and Study page includes a number of devotional Bible study methods.

DEVOTIONAL BIBLE STUDY

Devotional Bible Study is the logical gathering and examination of facts discovered in Scripture, arriving at conclusions based on those facts, and then applying what you have learned in your own life. As part of your exciting adventure in God's Word, you may incorporate simple devotional Bible study into your quiet time. Define one key word in the Greek or Hebrew or look up one cross-reference.

DEFINING AND UNDERSTANDING WORDS IN THE BIBLE

Because the Old Testament is written in Hebrew and the New Testament is written in Greek, scholars have devoted their life's work to producing invaluable study tools so that those who do not know Greek and Hebrew may understand the beauty of the original Biblical languages. These tools are so simple to use. The joy of discovery will be yours as you begin to look up the meanings of words in an Exhaustive Concordance (KJV, NASB, NIV) or the *NASB Hebrew-Greek Key Word Study Bible*. (More information on these tools in Chapter 5).

USING AN EXHAUSTIVE CONCORDANCE

1. *Word & Verse*: Find the word you wish to define in the main part of the concordance. Words are listed in alphabetical order. Under the word you wish to define are all the verses containing that word. Find the verse from your passage of study.

2. *Strong's Number*: To the right of your verse, there is a number. This is called the Strong's number. Record this number on your Read and Study page. Every Hebrew and Greek word is assigned a Strong's number. Many word study tools are keyed to this Strong's number.

3. *Definition*: After you have discovered the Strong's number, look in the back of the concordance in the Hebrew dictionary for words from the Old Testament or the Greek dictionary for words found in the New Testament. Find the number that was listed next to your word, and you will find the definition for your word. Write this definition on your Read and Study Page.

USING THE NASB HEBREW GREEK KEY WORD STUDY BIBLE

1. Locate the Bible passage and verse you are studying, identifying the Strong's number.

2. If the word you have chosen is underlined and the Strong's number above it is in bold, you

may look in Zodhiates' lexical aids (dictionary) in the Appendix (New or Old Testament lexical aids) using the Strong's number. The Lexical Aids contain very comprehensive definitions of the Hebrew and Greek words.

3. If the word you have chosen is not underlined and the Strong's number above it is not bold, use the second dictionary contained in *The NASB Hebrew-Greek Key Word Study Bible. (*This is the same dictionary as found at the back of the Exhaustive Concordance.) Numbers above words not in bold are only in the Strong's Dictionary found at the back of this Word Study Bible.

HOW TO CROSS-REFERENCE A VERSE

Cross-referencing a verse means that you would like to look up one or more verses that relate to your significant observation and shed light on its meaning.

1. Find the verse containing your significant observation in your Cross-Reference Bible. A cross-reference Bible will have lists of verse references in the sides or center margins.

2. If you have chosen a word or phrase for your significant observation, look directly above that word or phrase, and you will see a letter (e.g. "a, b, c…").

3. In the margin with additional references, find your verse reference, then the corresponding letter for your word, or phrase. You will find other Scripture references listed under that letter. Choose one or more references to read.

4. Record references on your Read and Study page.

5. Look up one or more references and record your insights on the Read and Study page.

Looking up the meanings of words (Exhaustive Concordance and *The NASB Hebrew-Greek Key Word Study Bible*) and Cross Reference Study are simply two methods of devotional Bible study. For even more devotional Bible study, see *Knowing and Loving The Bible* and *The Devotional Bible Study Notebook*.

READ & STUDY GOD'S WORD

"Study this book of the Law continually.
Meditate on it day and night..." — Joshua 1:8 NLT

SIX SECRETS TO A POWERFUL QUIET TIME ©2005

Date ___01-05-13___ Today's Scripture ___James 1:1-3___

Read God's Word — Record One Significant Observation

The testing of my faith produces endurance.

Immediate Context   This passage is all about trials!

Insights — Word Meanings — Cross-References

Insight — trials can be productive

Endurance - 5281 - hupomone - the quality that does not surrender under circumstances or succumb under trial

1 Peter 1:6-7 the proof of my faith is more precious than gold and will result in praise and glory at the revelation of Christ

Summary & Conclusions

It is possible to have joy in trials. A trial makes me stronger so that I won't surrender to adverse circumstances.

Application In My Life

This gives me the strength to stand strong in the current trial. Lord, help me see your perspective in the difficult circumstances of life.

ADORE GOD IN PRAYER

Prayer is your response to God's overtures, His Presence, and His involvement with you as you study His Word. Turn your thoughts to the Lord, lifting your soul to commune and converse with Him.

Adoration: Spend time in silence before God. Meditate on what you have learned about God and His works today. Worship and praise Him.

Confession: As you draw near to God, confess any sin that He brings to your mind. By faith, thank Him for His forgiveness and cleansing by the blood of Jesus Christ (1 John 1:9). Ask Him to fill you with His Holy Spirit (Ephesians 5:18).

Thanksgiving: Review God's blessings toward you, and offer Him thanksgiving for all He has done on your behalf (Psalm 95:2, Colossians 4:2).

Supplication: Turn to your daily prayer requests, using them as a reminder and guideline for making your requests known to the Lord. As you pray, add any new requests. Be sure to record all the ways God responds to you and answers your prayers.

How can you cultivate a life of prayer? When you talk with God, keep your Bible open, allowing God's Word to determine the nature and direction of your prayers. Meditate on the Psalms to learn how to pray. Vary your posture in prayer by sitting, stand, kneeling, or even lying facedown before the Lord. During difficulties, draw near to the Lord, patiently waiting for Him. God is pleased when you act upon what you know to be true. He will incline to you and hear your cry. Use your Adore God in Prayer pages as simple reminders of those things you would like to bring before God.

1. As you organize your Prayer Requests, think through names of people and topics such as family members, friends, disciples, personal requests, special requests, ministry, world, country, government leaders, church, church leadership, daily activities, schedule, and special interests. You may choose to pray through these requests on a daily or weekly basis.

2. Record each topic or person at the top of your prayer pages next to *Prayer For*_____.

3. Write out prayer requests for each of your topics as you begin to use your Adore God In Prayer pages in your quiet time. Always record the date of your requests. The "topic" subheading in the prayer requests boxes may be used for names/topics when your prayer page is a general topic such as "Church" or "Pastors." Write out your request, making it as specific as possible. You may wish to include Bible verses/promises related to your requests. As you pray, record any answers to prayer.

Optional Prayer Resources: To pray for people and nations in the world, see *Operation World* by Jason Mandryk (IVP Books 2012) operationworld.org. For praying Scripture, consult the *Praying God Will* series by Lee Roberts (Nashville, TN: Thomas Nelson 1993).

Prayer for __Bible Study__

Date: 6-20-2012   Topic: **Revelation study**
Scripture: Deuteronomy 31:8
Request: Father, prepare our hearts for our study this coming year.
Transform our lives with Your Word this year
Answer:

Date: 8-30-2012   Topic: **my teaching**
Scripture: James 1:5
Request: Lord, please give me wisdom as I study and prepare to teach.
Give me a listening ear, sensitive to Your guidance.
Answer:

Date: 9-15-2012   Topic: **class**
Scripture: Acts 17:11
Request: Lord, put it in the hearts of the students to study hard,
seeking you with all their hearts and souls.
Answer: 9-30-2012 Thank You Lord for these great students

Date: 10-1-2012   Topic: **prophecy**
Scripture: John 16:13
Request: Give us understanding into the prophecy of Daniel, especially
the 70 weeks.
Answer: 10-15-2012 Thank You for showing us Daniel 9:25-27

Date: 10-20-2012   Topic: **encouragement**
Scripture: Romans 15:4
Request: Lord, will you give encouragement and hope to those who are
discouraged right now?
Answer:

YIELD, ENJOY, REST

As you close your quiet time, spend a few moments reflecting on these vital applications of biblical truth in your relationship with God.

YIELD YOURSELF TO GOD

Place any unfulfilled dreams and desires in the hands of the Lord. Submit to God and His ways in your life today. Ask Him to teach you His ways, fill you with His Spirit, and give you His eternal perspective in relation to your present circumstances. If you sense a particular need today to humble yourself under God's mighty hand, that he may lift you up in due time (I Peter 5:6), write a brief prayer expressing what is on your heart. You will discover that God's thoughts and ways are higher than your thoughts and ways (Isaiah 55:8-9). Yielding yourself to God is an opportunity for you to surrender to the thoughts and ways of the Lord.

ENJOY HIS PRESENCE

Place today's responsibilities, activities, and appointments in the hands of the Lord. Record any special prayer requests related to your day. Write one significant insight the Lord gave you today in your quiet time to think about throughout the day. As you leave this quiet time and place of prayer, remember that the Lord goes with you. Talk to Him unceasingly, and share every experience of life with Him. He loves you. (1 Thessalonians 5:16-18, Matthew 28:20)

REST IN HIS LOVE

As you close your time with the Lord, place any anxious thoughts, conflicts, or difficult circumstances in the hands of the Lord. Record a promise or verse from God's Word related to your particular need. As you bask in the vast ocean of God's love, you will experience the surpassing riches of His grace and kindness. Your goal is to remain in His love. The result is rest and refreshment, producing within you a life glorifying to God. (Romans 8:38-40, Jeremiah 32:17, 26-27, Matthew 11:28-30, John 15:9).

YIELD — ENJOY — REST

"...let us run with perseverance the race marked out for us. Let us fix our eyes on Jesus, the author and perfecter of our faith..." — Hebrews 12:1-2 NIV

SIX SECRETS TO A POWERFUL QUIET TIME ©2005

Date <u>January 10, 2013.</u>

As you close your quiet time, spend a few moments in reflection — applying the truth of the Word of God in your own relationship with the Lord.

Yield Yourself to God

Place any unfulfilled dreams and desires in the hands of the Lord. If you sense a particular need today to humble yourself under God's mighty hand, that he may lift you up in due time (1 Peter 5:6), write a brief prayer expressing all that is on your heart.

Lord, keep my dreams and desires within the boundaries of your plans. Enable me to be faithful and reflect You to those around me.

Enjoy His Presence

Place today's activities, appointments, and responsibilities in the hands of the Lord.

Special Requests for Today —

Boldness from the Holy Spirit as I share my testimony.

One Significant Insight to Think About Today —

God wants me to dwell on eternal truths found in His Word.

Rest in His Love

As you close your time with the Lord, place any anxious thoughts, conflicts, or difficult circumstances in the hands of the Lord. record a promise or verse from God's Word related to your particular need.

Philippians 4:13 I can do everything through Him who gives me strength.

REFERENCE STUDY

Recommended Tools: Cross-reference Bible, *The Quiet Time Notebook*, Exhaustive Concordance
Optional Tools: *Treasury Of Scripture Knowledge, Thompson Chain Reference Bible, Nave's Topical Bible, NASB Hebrew-Greek Key Word Study Bible, Linguistic Key To The Greek New Testament*

You may use the Reference Study pages to study cross-references for any verse or topic in the Bible. As you read through a passage of Scripture, a word, phrase, verse, or topic will impress you. If you desire to look at other verses in the Bible related to this word, phrase, verse, or topic, you may choose to do a Reference Study.

1. Write out the verse or topic you have chosen to explore.

2. Reference Study of a Verse using a Reference Study page:

a. Note in your Cross-Reference Bible that each phrase within the verse has a corresponding letter above the beginning of phrase (a, b, c, …).

b. Look in center or side margin of Cross-Reference Bible, locating the chapter and verse you have chosen.

c. After you have located the correct chapter and verse in the margin containing other scripture references, look for the letters corresponding to each phrase within your verse. Select the letter for the phrase you wish to investigate, then record all the listed verses in the spaces provided on the Reference Study page. These verses you write are called cross-references. (Note: You may select more than one phrase, especially if you wish to look at all the cross-references related to the entire verse.) For additional cross-references, consult the *Treasury of Scripture Knowledge* or the *Thompson Chain Reference Bible*. This study page allows for up to 8 references. You may use more than one Reference Study page for your cross-references related to a single verse.

3. Topical Study using the Reference Study page:

a. Note that verses related to a topic do not always contain the actual word (such as "faith" or "love") in them. For example, a verse on the topic of love may actually use the English word, compassion or lovingkindness.

b. First, cross-reference any verses related to your topic in your chosen passage of Scripture (i.e. Reference Study of a verse).

c. Use your Exhaustive Concordance or the concordance in the back of your Bible to look up your topic such as "faith" or "love." Write any relevant verses in space provided on Reference Study page.

d. Use *Nave's Topical Bible* or the *Thompson Chain Reference Bible* to discover additional verses related to your topic.

4. Begin looking up each verse in your Reference or Topical study, one at a time, recording

what you learn from each verse and how it sheds light on meaning of original verse or topic. As you read each verse, briefly scan the surrounding verses to keep context in mind. In some cases, you will want to cross-reference one of these additional verses. If so, simply write any additional verses and insights in space provided.

5. As you look at each verse, there may be occasions that you would like to look up the definitions of some words. If so, simply use one of your word study tools to define the word. Then, write a brief definition in space provided on Reference Study page. Use the *Hebrew-Greek Key Word Study Bible*, or the *Linguistic Key To The Greek New Testament* (for New Testament words) to quickly look up word definitions.

6. After you have explored each reference, summarize what you have learned in 2-3 sentences. How do these verses shed light on your original verse or topic? (Note: If you are doing this study in conjunction with your daily Bible study, you may desire to record your conclusions and application on your Read and Study page.)

7. Write in 1-2 sentences how you will apply what you have learned to your life. (You may want to refer to the application questions found in the Read and Study God's Word instructions.)

For individual Reference Studies, choose from the following verses or topics:

Reference Study of a Verse: Deuteronomy 4:29, Jeremiah 29:11-12, John 14:21, 14:23, Acts 1:8, Romans 5:8, 8:38-39, 2 Corinthians 4:7, Ephesians 1:11, Philippians 2:8, 3:14, 4:6-7, Hebrews 1:3, 4:12, 5:7-8, James 4:8, I Peter 1:7, 4:19, Revelation 1:7.

Topical Study: God's Love, God's Glory, Fear of God, Jesus The Son of God, The Holy Spirit, Angels, Suffering, Humility, Hope, Love, Grace, The Church, Children, Blessing, Faith, Prayer, Righteousness, Man, Money and Riches, Sin, Word of God, Worship.

Verse–Topic ___Faith___ *Scripture* ___Hebrews 11:1___

Record observations and insights from the following references related to the selected verse or topic. Define any key words.

Key Words–Definitions

Faith—confidence in divine truth (Taken from Key Word Study Bible)

2 Samuel 22:31
Reference
God's way is perfect—He is a refuge (buckler KJV) for those who trust Him.

Psalm 51:1
Reference
When I trust (put my faith in) God, I can rejoice—He will defend me.

Psalm 9:10
Reference
Knowing God's name (His ways and character) will help me trust.

Romans 1:17
Reference
I am to live by faith.

Romans 5:1
_____
Reference

I am justified by faith and, as a result, I am given peace through Christ.

Romans 10:17
_____
Reference

Faith comes from hearing, and hearing from the Word of Christ.

1 Corinthians 2:5
_____
Reference

My faith does not rest in the wisdom of men, but the power of God.

Ephesians 6:16
_____
Reference

Faith is my shield in spiritual warfare.

Summary—Conclusions

1. Trust in God demonstrates my faith.
2. I am to live by faith.
3. Faith comes from hearing the word of Christ.
4. If I want to have faith, I must be in the Word, and come to know God and His ways.
5. Faith is a powerful weapon in spiritual warfare.

Application in My Life

Lord, today I see how important my demonstration of faith and trust in You is. I see the importance of knowing You in Your Word. Help me to make Your Word a priority.

NOTES

Recommended Tools: The Quiet Time Notebook

Optional Tools: Selected Books, Video and Audio books and messages, Magazines, *The Bible Background Commentary, International Standard Bible Encyclopedia, Expositor's Bible Commentary, New Bible Dictionary, New Bible Commentary*

As you spend time with God in His Word, you may want to do further reading to enhance your study. There will also be occasions when you will want to write down the most important points from lectures and sermons heard at a Bible study, conferences, retreats, or church. This Notes section is a convenient and valuable tool to record what you learn.

Book Study: Record Title, Date, Author, and related Subject/Scripture. As you read your selected book, write down quotes and important principles (include page numbers) on the Notes page. Write how what you have learned applies to your life.

Commentary Study: Record Title of Commentary, Date, Author, related Subject/Scripture. When studying a passage of Scripture, you may want to consult commentaries, dictionaries, or encyclopedias to learn what other scholars have reaped from their own study. Use *The Bible Background Commentary* to learn about the backgrounds of passages in the Bible. Use *Expositor's Bible Commentary, New Bible Commentary,* or any other commentaries including those found in study Bibles to learn more about any verse or passage in the Bible. Use the *International Standard Bible Encyclopedia, New Bible Dictionary* or any other selected Bible encyclopedia, dictionary, or Bible handbook to learn more about selected topics, characters, doctrines, or ethics. Record what you learn in the space provided (include page numbers). Write how what you have learned applies to your life.

Sermons, Lectures, Multimedia Messages: Use the Notes pages to record notes from any church sermons, lectures, conferences, Bible studies or audio/video messages. Write down the title of message, date, and speaker/teacher. Record the most important points. Also write out any ideas for further study. Always summarize what you have learned in 1-2 sentences, then think through how what you have learned applies to your life.

Articles and Blogs: You will discover wonderful insights from various articles and blogs found in Christian magazines and on the internet. Use the Notes section to record important quotes, insights, and applications in your life.

Note: Quiet Time Ministries has DVD, Downloadable M4V video, and Downloadable MP3 audio messages on many topics to help you grow in your relationship with the Lord. For more information on these and other quiet time resources, you may go online to The Quiet Time Online Store at quiettime.org or call Quiet Time Ministries at 1-800-925-6458.

"Be diligent to present yourself approved to God as a workman who does not need to be ashamed, handling accurately the word of truth." — 2 Timothy 2:15 NASB

SIX SECRETS TO A POWERFUL QUIET TIME ©2005

Date ___01-05-13___ Subject–Scripture ___Hebrews 11:1___

Title ___New Bible Commentary___ Author–Speaker ___Peterson___

Notes

New Bible Commentary ed. Carson, France, Motyer, Wenham (Downers Grove, IL: InterVarsity Press 1994), page 1346.

The writer is emphasizing the similarity between OT believers and Christians today waiting for the fulfillment of God's purposes. A comprehensive picture of faith. Hebrews shows the link between faith, hope, endurance, and obedience. God-honouring faith takes God at His Word and lives expectantly and obediently in the present, waiting for Him to fulfill His promises. Faith deals with things future and unseen. The reality of what we hope for is confirmed for us in our experience when we live by faith in God's promises. Our faith "proves" or "tests" the invisible realities such as God's existence, faithfulness to His Word, and His control over our world and its affairs.

Application In My Life

How exciting a life of faith is! I can see that God wants me to be confident and expectant of Him even in my present circumstances.

ENRICHING YOUR QUIET TIME

Draw near to God and He will draw near to you.

JAMES 4:8

There are so many ways to use *The Quiet Time Notebook* in your quiet time. The time you have to spend with the Lord will depend on the seasons of your life and your growth in your relationship with the Lord. Sometimes you may only have 10 minutes. Other times, you may have 30 minutes or even an hour. And occasionally, you may have enough time to draw near to God for a retreat of two or more hours. Following are some examples of the kind of variety that is possible in your quiet time. Experiment with these different examples and allow the Lord to teach you and lead you as you draw near to Him.

10 MINUTE QUIET TIME

Prepare Your Heart—Pray a simple prayer asking the Lord to quiet your heart.

Read And Study God's Word—Read the Bible using your Bible reading plan. Write one insight or significant verse from your reading on a Prepare Your Heart journal page.

Adore God In Prayer—Talk with God using selected Adore God in Prayer pages as written reminders of your requests.

Yield, Enjoy, Rest—Reflect on these important areas using a Yield, Enjoy, Rest page as you close your time with the Lord.

20 MINUTE QUIET TIME

Prepare Your Heart—Selected reading from devotional book such as *My Utmost For His Highest.*

Read And Study God's Word—Read the Bible using your Bible reading plan. Write one insight or significant verse from your reading on a Prepare Your Heart journal page.

Adore God In Prayer—Talk with God using selected Adore God in Prayer pages as written reminders of your requests.

Yield, Enjoy, Rest—Reflect on these important areas using a Yield, Enjoy, Rest page as you close your time with the Lord.

30 MINUTE QUIET TIME

Prepare Your Heart—Read selected Psalm from the Psalm reading plan (see Chapter 6) or read some selected devotional reading. Write any insights or significant observations on the Prepare Your Heart journal page.

Read And Study God's Word—Read the Bible using your Bible reading plan. Write your insights on a Read and Study page in your Quiet Time Notebook.

Adore God In Prayer—Talk with God using selected Adore God in Prayer pages as written reminders of your requests. Yield, Enjoy, Rest—Reflect on these important areas using a Yield, Enjoy, Rest page as you close your time with the Lord.

60 MINUTE QUIET TIME

Prepare Your Heart—Read selected Psalm for the day from the Psalm Reading Plan (see Chapter 6) and read selected devotional reading from a favorite devotional. Write your insights and a prayer on the Prepare Your Heart journal page.

Read And Study God's Word—Read the Bible using your Bible reading plan. Choose one significant insight and write it on your Read and Study page. Use the Read and Study page to dig deeper with devotional Bible study.

Adore God In Prayer—Talk with God using selected Adore God in Prayer pages as written reminders of your requests.

Yield, Enjoy, Rest—Reflect on these important areas and write your thoughts on the Yield, Enjoy, Rest page as you close your time with the Lord.

2 HOUR QUIET TIME RETREAT

Prepare Your Heart—Read selected Psalm for the day from the Psalm Bible Reading Plan (see Chapter 6). Read from devotional books such as *My Utmost For His Highest* and/or *The Pursuit of God*. Write your insights on the Prepare Your Heart Journal page. Worship the Lord using your hymnbook or worship music.

Read And Study God's Word—Read the Bible using your Bible reading plan. Choose one significant insight and write it on your Read and Study page. Use the Read and Study page to dig deeper with devotional Bible study. Optional: Reference study or read from selected commentaries.

Adore God In Prayer—Talk with God using the Adore God in Prayer pages as written reminders of your requests.

Yield, Enjoy, Rest—Reflect on these important areas in this section as you close your time with the Lord. Write your thoughts on the Yield, Enjoy, Rest page. You may close your retreat by writing a prayer on a Prepare Your Heart Journal page.

TEN SIMPLE WAYS TO ENRICH YOUR QUIET TIME

There are many ways to vary your quiet time so that it is richer and deeper. Here are ten ways to enrich your quiet time.

- Meditate on a Psalm or Proverb in a translation such as The New Living Translation or the New International Version and write your thoughts in your journal.

- Vary your location. Take your Bible and *The Quiet Time Notebook* to a park, mountains, beach, or favorite restaurant.

- Share your quiet time with a close friend. Read through a passage of Scripture together and exchange insights. Share reflections from devotional reading.

- Read from a biography of a Christian who walked closely with the Lord.

- Meditate on a book from the Devotional Reading list (see Chapter 5).

- Listen to some new Praise or Worship music, meditate on the words, and worship the Lord.

- Choose a passage of Scripture from any of the Bible Reading Plans (see Chapter 6) and dig deeper in Devotional Bible Study with a Reference Study.

- Listen to a message from a favorite Bible teacher and write out what you learn on the Notes page.

- Go for a walk, sharing with the Lord along the way.

- Choose a favorite passage of Scripture and spend your quiet time memorizing it. Think about each phrase and its meaning in your life throughout the day.

GETTING STARTED IN YOUR QUIET TIME

*Do you not know that those who run in a race all run, but only one
receives the prize? Run in such a way that you may win.*

1 CORINTHIANS 9:24

Planning and preparation will make a difference in your quiet time. Paul encourages us to run in such a way that we may win (1 Corinthians 9:24). His point is clear. Being intentional and focused are important in our life if we desire to glorify God. Now that you have learned more about how to use *The Quiet Time Notebook*, let's take some time and get organized for your quiet time. Use the following Quiet Time Worksheet to prepare for your quiet time.

QUIET TIME WORKSHEET

1. Ask God to lead and guide you as you plan for quiet time alone with Him. Write a prayer to the Lord expressing all that is on your heart.

2. As you plan for your daily quiet time, spend a few moments evaluating what God has taught you during this past year.

2. What do you desire in your relationship with God? Write out your commitment to the Lord to seek Him, know Him, and spend consistent time alone with Him.

3. Choose a time and a place for your quiet time. Organize your quiet time area and keep all your materials together in one place.

Time_____

Place_____

3. Choose some books and daily devotional reading to use as you Prepare Your Heart in your quiet times this year. A list of suggested reading is included later in this chapter (see Your Quiet Time Library). Books I'd like to use in my quiet time this year:

4. To Read and Study God's Word, decide how you will stay in God's Word on a daily basis this year by choosing a Bible Reading Plan. Refer to Chapter 6 "Choose A Bible Reading Plan" to make your choice. My Bible Reading Plan this year will be:

5. Evaluate your present devotional materials. Make a list of Bible study tools to obtain in the future as an investment in your relationship with the Lord. (See "Your Quiet Time Library" for description of tools.) You will be able to use this quiet time notebook in your quiet time even if you do not have all these tools. Resources For Your Daily Quiet Time include a Cross-Reference Bible, *The Quiet Time Notebook*, Devotional Reading, Praise/Worship music, Hymnbook, *NASB Hebrew-Greek Key Word Study Bible*, and Exhaustive Concordance.

Bible Study Tools I Have:

Future Bible Study Tools:

6. Organize your prayer requests to Adore God In Prayer. You may desire to pray to the Lord weekly for certain requests and daily for others.

Daily Prayer Requests:

Weekly Prayer Requests:
Sunday:
Monday:
Tuesday:
Wednesday:
Thursday:
Friday:
Saturday:

7. Use Reflect On Your Quiet Time This Month pages in Chapter 7 for quiet time evaluation as desired.

8. Ask God for a verse and a word for this year to focus on in your relationship with the Lord. Write the Verse and Word here and in the front of your Quiet Time Notebook.
Verse:

Word:

YOUR QUIET TIME LIBRARY

A good Bible Study tool or devotional book is always a lifetime investment and is worthwhile for your spiritual growth. The following is a list of recommended Bible Study tools and Devotional Reading books. These recommended Bible Study tools will enrich your quiet time over the years as you learn how to use them with the inductive studies contained in this notebook. They will also give you maximum use of this Quiet Time Notebook.

RECOMMENDED BIBLE STUDY TOOLS

- *New American Standard Bible - Cross-Reference Edition* (La Habra, CA: Lockman Foundation, 1960) or *The Holy Bible: New International Version - Cross- Reference Edition* (Grand Rapids, MI: Zondervan Bible Publishers, 1988).

- *NASB Exhaustive Concordance* by Robert L. Thomas ed. (Nashville, TN: Holman Bible Publishers, 1981) or

- *NIV Exhaustive Concordance* (Grand Rapids, MI: Zondervan Publishers).

- *The NASB Hebrew-Greek Key Word Study Bible* by Spiros Zodhiates ed. (Chattanooga, TN: AMG Publishers, 1990) or The Complete Word Study New Testament and The Complete Word Study Old Testament by Spiros Zodhiates ed. (Chattanooga, TN: AMG Publishers, 1990 and 1994).

- *The Treasury Of Scripture Knowledge* by Jerome H. Smith ed. (Nashville, TN: Thomas Nelson Reference 1992).

RECOMMENDED DEVOTIONAL READING

As part of your preparation of heart when you begin your quiet time, you may choose to read and reflect on a small portion of a classic devotional book. You may choose from among the following books or from the books in your own library.

Abide In Christ by Andrew Murray from The Andrew Murray Collection (Uhrichsville, OH: Barbour & Company, Inc., 1985).

Daily Light Devotional NKJV by Anne Graham Lotz (Nashville, TN: Thomas Nelson Publishing Co. 1998)

The Edges Of His Ways by Amy Carmichael (Fort Washington, PA: Christian Literature Crusade, 1984).

Knowing God by J.I. Packer (Downers Grove, Illinois: InterVarsity Press, 1973).

Morning And Evening by Charles Haddon Spurgeon (New Kensington, PA: Whitaker House 2001)

My Utmost For His Highest by Oswald Chambers (New York, NY: Dodd, Mead, & Company, 1935).

The Pursuit Of God by A.W. Tozer (Camp Hill, PA: Christian Publications Inc., 1982).

Springs in the Valley by Mrs. Charles E. Cowman

Streams in the Desert by Mrs. Charles E. Cowman

Thirty-One Days Of Praise by Ruth Myers (Sisters, OR: Multnomah Books, 1994).

MY PRAYER FOR YOU

Lord Jesus, I pray for this one who desires to know You more and grow in their relationship with You. They have The Quiet Time Notebook and are ready to embark on this great adventure of knowing You. I ask that You will lead them in their quiet time, and draw them close to Your heart. Will You give them a deep passion for you through the power of the Holy Spirit. Teach them powerful truths in Your Word and lead them as they draw near to You in prayer. Transform their hearts, more and more with each passing day, making them the person You want them to be. May they glorify You, and may they walk wholeheartedly with You every day of their life on earth. And may they someday hear those wonderful words from You when they see You face to face: "Well done, good and faithful servant." In Jesus' Name, Amen.

YOUR BIBLE READING PLAN

*Let the word of Christ richly dwell within you, with all wisdom
teaching and admonishing one another with psalms and hymns and
spiritual songs, singing with thankfulness in your hearts to God.*

COLOSSIANS 3:16

Because you want to be in the Word of God on a consistent basis, it is necessary to have an organized plan for choosing a portion of the Bible to read and study each day. Read through each of these choices carefully, ask God for His wisdom in choosing one of these reading plans, and then decide what you would like to use this year. You may even want to go to a Christian bookstore to examine the different Daily Devotional Bibles and other materials mentioned. Once you have made your decision, mark the box in pencil so that you will have a reminder of your choice. Each day you will use your selected Bible Reading Plan to read and study a portion of Scripture. One of the greatest obstacles in a person's quiet time is the difficulty in deciding where to even start reading in the Bible. Choosing a Bible Reading Plan eliminates this obstacle. Feel free to be sensitive to the Lord's leading in changing your reading plan from time to time, and from year to year. Your daily passage should come from one of the following:

- One of the 2 daily reading plans found later in this chapter: Read Through The Bible In A Year or Read Through Psalms And Proverbs Twice A Year

- Choose a book of the Bible and read 1 chapter a day.

- Daily Devotional Bibles—Some of the most popular Daily Devotional Bibles include the *NIV Men's/Women's Devotional Bible* (Grand Rapids, Michigan: Zondervan Publishing House, 1990—this devotional Bible covers Genesis to Revelation in 1 year and contains daily devotional readings written by well-known men and women), *The One Year Bible*—in NIV, NASB, or NLT, (Wheaton, Illinois: Tyndale House Publishers, 1988—this devotional Bible offers a daily portion of Scripture from the Old and New Testaments, a Psalm, and a Proverb and covers the entire Bible in a year), *The Daily Bible*—NIV with commentary by F. LaGard Smith (Eugene, Oregon: Harvest House Publishers, 1984—his unique devotional Bible takes you through the Bible in a year with daily readings in chronological order. Included are brief introductions to many of the readings, providing excellent context for your study), and *The Daily Walk Bible*—NIV, NLT (Wheaton, Illinois: Tyndale House Publishers—this devotional Bible, with reading from Genesis to Revelation includes introductions and outlines for every book of the Bible).

- Devotional Reading Guides—Daily Walk, Closer Walk, Tapestry, or Quiet Walk by Walk Through The Bible Ministries available at walkthru.org. These daily Bible reading guides include Scripture and devotional insights. In Touch Magazine by Charles Stanley's In Touch Ministries available at intouch.org. Includes daily Bible readings and commentary by pastor and teacher, Dr. Charles Stanley. Tabletalk by R.C. Sproul's Ligonier Ministries available at ligonier.org. Includes daily Bible readings, commentary by teacher and theologian, Dr. R.C. Sproul.

- Ongoing Bible Study—If you are involved in an ongoing Bible study, you may choose to complete that study in place of using the *Read and Study* section in your Quiet Time Notebook. Ongoing Bible studies may include Quiet Time Bible studies from Quiet Time Ministries available at quiettime.org, Precept Bible studies available at precept.org, Lifeway Bible studies available at lifeway.com, and Bible Study Fellowship.

READ THROUGH THE PSALMS AND PROVERBS

January		*February*		*March*		*April*	
1	Psalm 1	1	Psalm 32	1	Psalm 60	1	Psalm 91
2	Psalm 2	2	Psalm 33	2	Psalm 61	2	Psalm 92
3	Psalm 3	3	Psalm 34	3	Psalm 62	3	Psalm 93
4	Psalm 4	4	Psalm 35	4	Psalm 63	4	Psalm 94
5	Psalm 5	5	Psalm 36	5	Psalm 64	5	Psalm 95
6	Psalm 6	6	Psalm 37	6	Psalm 65	6	Psalm 96
7	Psalm 7	7	Psalm 38	7	Psalm 66	7	Psalm 97
8	Psalm 8	8	Psalm 39	8	Psalm 67	8	Psalm 98
9	Psalm 9	9	Psalm 40	9	Psalm 68	9	Psalm 99
10	Psalm 10	10	Psalm 41	10	Psalm 69	10	Psalm 100
11	Psalm 11	11	Psalm 42	11	Psalm 70	11	Psalm 101
12	Psalm 12	12	Psalm 43	12	Psalm 71	12	Psalm 102
13	Psalm 13	13	Psalm 44	13	Psalm 72	13	Psalm 103
14	Psalm 14	14	Psalm 45	14	Psalm 73	14	Psalm 104
15	Psalm 15	15	Psalm 46	15	Psalm 74	15	Psalm 105
16	Psalm 16	16	Psalm 47	16	Psalm 75	16	Psalm 106
17	Psalm 17	17	Psalm 48	17	Psalm 76	17	Psalm 107
18	Psalm 18	18	Psalm 49	18	Psalm 77	18	Psalm 108
19	Psalm 19	19	Psalm 50	19	Psalm 78	19	Psalm 109
20	Psalm 20	20	Psalm 51	20	Psalm 79	20	Psalm 110
21	Psalm 21	21	Psalm 52	21	Psalm 80	21	Psalm 111
22	Psalm 22	22	Psalm 53	22	Psalm 81	22	Psalm 112
23	Psalm 23	23	Psalm 54	23	Psalm 82	23	Psalm 113
24	Psalm 24	24	Psalm 55	24	Psalm 83	24	Psalm 114
25	Psalm 25	25	Psalm 56	25	Psalm 84	25	Psalm 115
26	Psalm 26	26	Psalm 57	26	Psalm 85	26	Psalm 116
27	Psalm 27	27	Psalm 58	27	Psalm 86	27	Psalm 117
28	Psalm 28	28	Psalm 59	28	Psalm 87	28	Psalm 118
29	Psalm 29			29	Psalm 88	29	Psalm 119:1-88
30	Psalm 30			30	Psalm 89	30	Psalm 119:89-176
31	Psalm 31			31	Psalm 90		

READ THROUGH THE PSALMS AND PROVERBS

May		*June*		*July*		*August*	
1	Psalm 120	1	Proverbs 1	1	Proverbs 31	1	Psalm 31
2	Psalm 121	2	Proverbs 2	2	Psalm 1	2	Psalm 32
3	Psalm 122	3	Proverbs 3	3	Psalm 2	3	Psalm 33
4	Psalm 123	4	Proverbs 4	4	Psalm 3	4	Psalm 34
5	Psalm 124	5	Proverbs 5	5	Psalm 4	5	Psalm 35
6	Psalm 125	6	Proverbs 6	6	Psalm 5	6	Psalm 36
7	Psalm 126	7	Proverbs 7	7	Psalm 6	7	Psalm 37
8	Psalm 127	8	Proverbs 8	8	Psalm 7	8	Psalm 38
9	Psalm 128	9	Proverbs 9	9	Psalm 8	9	Psalm 39
10	Psalm 129	10	Proverbs 10	10	Psalm 9	10	Psalm 40
11	Psalm 130	11	Proverbs 11	11	Psalm 10	11	Psalm 41
12	Psalm 131	12	Proverbs 12	12	Psalm 11	12	Psalm 42
13	Psalm 132	13	Proverbs 13	13	Psalm 12	13	Psalm 43
14	Psalm 133	14	Proverbs 14	14	Psalm 13	14	Psalm 44
15	Psalm 134	15	Proverbs 15	15	Psalm 14	15	Psalm 45
16	Psalm 135	16	Proverbs 16	16	Psalm 15	16	Psalm 46
17	Psalm 136	17	Proverbs 17	17	Psalm 16	17	Psalm 47
18	Psalm 137	18	Proverbs 18	18	Psalm 17	18	Psalm 48
19	Psalm 138	19	Proverbs 19	19	Psalm 18	19	Psalm 49
20	Psalm 139	20	Proverbs 20	20	Psalm 19	20	Psalm 50
21	Psalm 140	21	Proverbs 21	21	Psalm 20	21	Psalm 51
22	Psalm 141	22	Proverbs 22	22	Psalm 21	22	Psalm 52
23	Psalm 142	23	Proverbs 23	23	Psalm 22	23	Psalm 53
24	Psalm 143	24	Proverbs 24	24	Psalm 23	24	Psalm 54
25	Psalm 144	25	Proverbs 25	25	Psalm 24	25	Psalm 55
26	Psalm 145	26	Proverbs 26	26	Psalm 25	26	Psalm 56
27	Psalm 146	27	Proverbs 27	27	Psalm 26	27	Psalm 57
28	Psalm 147	28	Proverbs 28	28	Psalm 27	28	Psalm 58
29	Psalm 148	29	Proverbs 29	29	Psalm 28	29	Psalm 59
30	Psalm 149	30	Proverbs 30	30	Psalm 29	30	Psalm 60
31	Psalm 150			31	Psalm 30	31	Psalm 61

READ THROUGH THE PSALMS AND PROVERBS

September		*October*		*November*		*December*	
1	Psalm 62	1	Psalm 92	1	Psalm 121	1	Proverbs 1
2	Psalm 63	2	Psalm 93	2	Psalm 122	2	Proverbs 2
3	Psalm 64	3	Psalm 94	3	Psalm 123	3	Proverbs 3
4	Psalm 65	4	Psalm 95	4	Psalm 124	4	Proverbs 4
5	Psalm 66	5	Psalm 96	5	Psalm 125	5	Proverbs 5
6	Psalm 67	6	Psalm 97	6	Psalm 126	6	Proverbs 6
7	Psalm 68	7	Psalm 98	7	Psalm 127	7	Proverbs 7
8	Psalm 69	8	Psalm 99	8	Psalm 128	8	Proverbs 8
9	Psalm 70	9	Psalm 100	9	Psalm 129	9	Proverbs 9
10	Psalm 71	10	Psalm 101	10	Psalm 130	10	Proverbs 10
11	Psalm 72	11	Psalm 102	11	Psalm 131	11	Proverbs 11
12	Psalm 73	12	Psalm 103	12	Psalm 132	12	Proverbs 12
13	Psalm 74	13	Psalm 104	13	Psalm 133	13	Proverbs 13
14	Psalm 75	14	Psalm 105	14	Psalm 134	14	Proverbs 14
15	Psalm 76	15	Psalm 106	15	Psalm 135	15	Proverbs 15
16	Psalm 77	16	Psalm 107	16	Psalm 136	16	Proverbs 16
17	Psalm 78	17	Psalm 108	17	Psalm 137	17	Proverbs 17
18	Psalm 79	18	Psalm 109	18	Psalm 138	18	Proverbs 18
19	Psalm 80	19	Psalm 110	19	Psalm 139	19	Proverbs 19
20	Psalm 81	20	Psalm 111	20	Psalm 140	20	Proverbs 20
21	Psalm 82	21	Psalm 112	21	Psalm 141	21	Proverbs 21
22	Psalm 83	22	Psalm 113	22	Psalm 142	22	Proverbs 22
23	Psalm 84	23	Psalm 114	23	Psalm 143	23	Proverbs 23
24	Psalm 85	24	Psalm 115	24	Psalm 144	24	Proverbs 24
25	Psalm 86	25	Psalm 116	25	Psalm 145	25	Proverbs 25
26	Psalm 87	26	Psalm 117	26	Psalm 146	26	Proverbs 26
27	Psalm 88	27	Psalm 118	27	Psalm 147	27	Proverbs 27
28	Psalm 89	28	119:1-64	28	Psalm 148	28	Proverbs 28
29	Psalm 90	29	119:65-120	29	Psalm 149	29	Proverbs 29
30	Psalm 91	30	119:121-176	30	Psalm 150	30	Proverbs 30
		31	Psalm 120			31	Proverbs 31

READ THROUGH THE BIBLE IN A YEAR

January		February		March		April	
1	Gen 1-3	1	Lev 11-14	1	Joshua 8-10	1	1 Kings 1-3
2	Gen 4-6	2	Lev 15-17	2	Joshua 11-13	2	1 Kings 4-7
3	Gen 7-9	3	Lev 18-20	3	Joshua 14-17	3	1 Kings 8-10
4	Gen 10-13	4	Lev 21-24	4	Joshua 18-21	4	1 Kings 11-14
5	Gen 14-17	5	Lev 25-27	5	Joshua 22-24	5	1 Kings 15-17
6	Gen 18-20	6	Num 1-4	6	Judges 1-3	6	1 Kings 18-20
7	Gen 21-23	7	Num 5-7	7	Judges 4-8	7	1 Kings 21-22
8	Gen 24-26	8	Num 8-10	8	Judges 9-10	8	2 Kings 1-4
9	Gen 27-30	9	Num 11-14	9	Judges 11-12	9	2 Kings 5-7
10	Gen 31-33	10	Num 15-17	10	Judges 13-16	10	2 Kings 8-10
11	Gen 34-36	11	Num 18-20	11	Judges 17-18	11	2 Kings 11-13
12	Gen 37-40	12	Num 21-23	12	Judges 19-21	12	2 Kings 14-17
13	Gen 41-45	13	Num 24-27	13	Ruth 1-4	13	2 Kings 18-20
14	Gen 46-48	14	Num 28-30	14	1 Sam 1-3	14	2 Kings 21-25
15	Gen 49-50	15	Num 31-33	15	1 Sam 4-7	15	1 Chron 1-4
16	Exodus 1-4	16	Num 34-36	16	1 Sam 8-10	16	1 Chron 5-8
17	Exodus 5-7	17	Deut 1-4	17	1 Sam 11-13	17	1 Chron 9-12
18	Exodus 8-11	18	Deut 5-7	18	1 Sam 14-16	18	1 Chron 13-16
19	Exodus 12-14	19	Deut 8-11	19	1 Sam 17-20	19	1 Chron 17-19
20	Exodus 15-17	20	Deut 12-14	20	1 Sam 21-23	20	1 Chron 20-22
21	Exodus 18-20	21	Deut 15-17	21	1 Sam 24-26	21	1 Chron 23-25
22	Exodus 21-23	22	Deut 18-20	22	1 Sam 27-29	22	1 Chron 26-29
23	Exodus 24-26	23	Deut 21-23	23	1 Sam 30-31	23	2 Chron 1-3
24	Exodus 27-29	24	Deut 24-26	24	2 Sam 1-3	24	2 Chron 4-7
25	Exodus 30-32	25	Deut 27-30	25	2 Sam 4-6	25	2 Chron 8-9
26	Exodus 33-35	26	Deut 31-34	26	2 Sam 7-9	26	2 Chron 10-12
27	Exodus 36-38	27	Joshua 1-4	27	2 Sam 10-12	27	2 Chron 13-15
28	Exodus 39-40	28	Joshua 5-7	28	2 Sam 13-15	28	2 Chron 16-18
29	Lev 1-4			29	2 Sam 16-19	29	2 Chron 19-21
30	Lev 5-7			30	2 Sam 20-22	30	2 Chron 22-24
31	Lev 8-10			31	2 Sam 23-24		

READ THROUGH THE BIBLE IN A YEAR

May		*June*		*July*		*August*	
1	2 Chron 25-28	1	Psalm 19-21	1	Psalm 115-118	1	Isaiah 13-16
2	2 Chron 29-32	2	Psalm 22-24	2	Psalm 119	2	Isaiah 17-20
3	2 Chron 33-36	3	Psalm 25-27	3	Psalm 120-123	3	Isaiah 21-23
4	Ezra 1-4	4	Psalm 28-30	4	Psalm 124-127	4	Isaiah 24-26
5	Ezra 5-7	5	Psalm 31-33	5	Psalm 128-131	5	Isaiah 27-29
6	Ezra 8-10	6	Psalm 34-36	6	Psalm 132-135	6	Isaiah 30-32
7	Neh 1-2	7	Psalm 37-39	7	Psalm 136-138	7	Isaiah 33-35
8	Neh 3-5	8	Psalm 40-42	8	Psalm 139-141	8	Isaiah 36-39
9	Neh 6-9	9	Psalm 43-46	9	Psalm 142-144	9	Isaiah 40-43
10	Neh 10-13	10	Psalm 47-50	10	Psalm 145-147	10	Isaiah 44-46
11	Esther 1-3	11	Psalm 51-54	11	Psalm 148-150	11	Isaiah 47-49
12	Esther 4-7	12	Psalm 55-57	12	Proverbs 1-3	12	Isaiah 50-52
13	Esther 8-10	13	Psalm 58-61	13	Proverbs 4-6	13	Isaiah 53-55
14	Job 1-3	14	Psalm 62-64	14	Proverbs 7-9	14	Isaiah 56-58
15	Job 4-7	15	Psalm 65-67	15	Proverbs 10-12	15	Isaiah 59-62
16	Job 8-10	16	Psalm 68-70	16	Proverbs 13-15	16	Isaiah 63-66
17	Job 11-14	17	Psalm 71-73	17	Proverbs 16-18	17	Jer 1-3
18	Job 15-17	18	Psalm 74-76	18	Proverbs 19-21	18	Jer 4-6
19	Job 18-20	19	Psalm 77-79	19	Proverbs 22-24	19	Jer 7-9
20	Job 21-24	20	Psalm 80-82	20	Proverbs 25-27	20	Jer 10-12
21	Job 25-28	21	Psalm 83-85	21	Proverbs 28-31	21	Jer 13-15
22	Job 29-31	22	Psalm 86-88	22	Ecc 1-3	22	Jer 16-17
23	Job 32-34	23	Psalm 89-91	23	Ecc 4-6	23	Jer 18-20
24	Job 35-37	24	Psalm 92-94	24	Ecc 7-9	24	Jer 21-23
25	Job 38-42	25	Psalm 95-97	25	Ecc 10-12	25	Jer 24-26
26	Psalm 1-3	26	Psalm 98-100	26	Song of Sol 1-4	26	Jer 27-29
27	Psalm 4-6	27	Psalm 101-103	27	Song of Sol 5-8	27	Jer 30-31
28	Psalm 7-9	28	Psalm 104-106	28	Isaiah 1-3	28	Jer 32-34
29	Psalm 10-12	29	Psalm 107-110	29	Isaiah 4-6	29	Jer 35-37
30	Psalm 13-15	30	Psalm 111-114	30	Isaiah 7-9	30	Jer 38-41
31	Psalm 16-18			31	Isaiah 10-12	31	Jer 42-44

READ THROUGH THE BIBLE IN A YEAR

September		*October*		*November*		*December*	
1	Jer 45-48	1	Jonah 1-4	1	John 1-3	1	Galatians 1-3
2	Jer 49-52	2	Micah 1-4	2	John 4-6	2	Galatians 4-6
3	Lam 1-5	3	Micah 5-7	3	John 7-9	3	Ephesians 1-3
4	Ezekiel 1-3	4	Nahum 1-3	4	John 10-13	4	Ephesians 4-6
5	Ezekiel 4-6	5	Hab 1-3	5	John 14-16	5	Philippians 1-4
6	Ezekiel 7-9	6	Zeph 1-3	6	John 17-21	6	Colossians 1-4
7	Ezekiel 10-12	7	Haggai 1-2	7	Acts 1-4	7	1 Thess 1-5
8	Ezekiel 13-15	8	Zech 1-4	8	Acts 5-7	8	2 Thess 1-3
9	Ezekiel 16-18	9	Zech 5-8	9	Acts 8-9	9	1 Timothy 1-3
10	Ezekiel 19-21	10	Zech 9-11	10	Acts 10-12	10	1 Timothy 4-6
11	Ezekiel 22-24	11	Zech 12-14	11	Acts 13-16	11	2 Timothy 1-4
12	Ezekiel 25-28	12	Malachi 1-4	12	Acts 17-20	12	Philemon
13	Ezekiel 29-32	13	Matthew 1-4	13	Acts 21-23	13	Hebrews 1-2
14	Ezekiel 33-36	14	Matthew 5-7	14	Acts 24-26	14	Hebrews 3-4
15	Ezekiel 37-39	15	Matthew 8-10	15	Acts 27-28	15	Hebrews 5-7
16	Ezekiel 40-43	16	Matthew 11-13	16	Romans 1-3	16	Hebrews 8-10
17	Ezekiel 44-48	17	Matthew 14-16	17	Romans 4-5	17	Hebrews 11
18	Daniel 1-3	18	Matthew 17-20	18	Romans 6-8	18	Hebrews 12-13
19	Daniel 4-6	19	Matthew 21-23	19	Romans 9-11	19	James 1-5
20	Daniel 7-9	20	Matthew 24-26	20	Romans 12-13	20	1 Peter 1-5
21	Daniel 10-12	21	Matthew 27-28	21	Romans 14-16	21	2 Peter 1-3
22	Hosea 1-3	22	Mark 1-4	22	1 Cor 1-3	22	1 John 1-5
23	Hosea 4-7	23	Mark 5-8	23	1 Cor 4-6	23	2 John-Jude
24	Hosea 8-10	24	Mark 9-12	24	1 Cor 7-9	24	Revelation 1-3
25	Hosea 11-14	25	Mark 13-16	25	1 Cor 10-12	25	Revelation 4-5
26	Joel 1-3	26	Luke 1-3	26	1 Cor 13-16	26	Revelation 6-9
27	Amos 1-3	27	Luke 4-6	27	2 Cor 1-3	27	Revelation 10-13
28	Amos 4-6	28	Luke 7-9	28	2 Cor 4-6	28	Revelation 14-16
29	Amos 7-9	29	Luke 10-12	29	2 Cor 7-9	29	Revelation 17-18
30	Obadiah	30	Luke 13-17	30	2 Cor 10-13	30	Revelation 19-20
		31	Luke 18-21			31	Revelation 21-22

MONTHLY QUIET TIME REFLECTION PAGES

But grow in the grace and knowledge of our Lord and Savior Jesus Christ.
To Him be the glory, both now and to the day of eternity. Amen.

2 PETER 3:18

Growing in grace is your privilege as a child of God. He has placed you in an environment that is perfectly conducive for spiritual growth. The environment is grace. Grace is the free, unmerited favor of God. You can't earn it. You don't deserve it. Grace is at the heart of all God does toward you, for you, and in you.[1] Grace finds you, saves you, and keeps you. Grace gives you everything you need, more than you could ever want, and places you in an eternal, secure, favorable position forever. You stand in grace, according to the apostle Paul (Romans 4:2). In your quiet time, you will experience God's grace, His amazing love in action. Just imagine His arms open wide to you, regardless of what you have done. Grace opens the floodgates and allows God's endless love to pour in your life, moment by moment, on into eternity.

So as you spend time day after day, month after month, and year after year, you are going to grow deeper in your relationship with God. Your heart is going to be transformed, and you will bear fruit for the glory of God. One of the practices that I have found to be effective in helping me grow in my walk with the Lord is to take some time every month or so, and reflect on all that God is teaching me. I encourage you to set aside special times with the Lord where you stop to review and reflect what God is doing in your life. You will be amazed at all He is teaching you, amazing ways He is answering your prayers, and the heart transformation and soul revival you are experiencing. And then, when you see it, you will stop, and say "Thank You, Lord."

Included are Instructions and twelve Monthly Quiet Time Reflection pages, enough to take you through a year of reflection on your journey with the Lord. Without a doubt, as I look back over the years, I can see how God has faithfully poured out mercy and grace and compassion on me through the most difficult seasons of my life. I can see that He is teaching me to trust Him and walk by faith, even when I am walking through the fog of adversity. I am learning to hold tightly to His promises and run with endurance the race that is set before me.

MONTHLY QUIET TIME REFLECTION GUIDE

I encourage you to schedule a time each month when you can sit alone with the Lord and talk with Him about all He is doing in your life. This is an opportunity for you to think about your quiet time, devotional reading, burdens for prayer, and victories in your relationship with Christ.

1. The Monthly Quiet Time Reflection page gives a space to write the current month. I encourage you to write the month and the year, i.e. October 2013.

2. You can use this page day by day to keep track of your quiet times. This is optional, but is a way to see when you spent time with the Lord and how consistent you are.

3. During your time of reflection, begin with prayer. Ask the Lord to speak to you as you draw near to Him.

4. Look back through your quiet times by looking at the pages you've used in *The Quiet Time Notebook* i.e. Prepare Your Heart Journal, Read and Study, Adore God in Prayer, and Yield, Enjoy, Rest.

5. Take time with each question, and write your insights and observations.

6. Close by writing out any additional thoughts and a prayer to the Lord.

REFLECT ON YOUR QUIET TIME THIS MONTH_____

_____Day 1	_____Day 11	_____Day 21
_____Day 2	_____Day 12	_____Day 22
_____Day 3	_____Day 13	_____Day 23
_____Day 4	_____Day 14	_____Day 24
_____Day 5	_____Day 15	_____Day 25
_____Day 6	_____Day 16	_____Day 26
_____Day 7	_____Day 17	_____Day 27
_____Day 8	_____Day 18	_____Day 28
_____Day 9	_____Day 19	_____Day 29
_____Day 10	_____Day 20	_____Day 30
		_____Day 31

What was the most significant insight from the Lord?

What was the most significant verse?

What was your favorite devotional reading?

What was the most significant answer to prayer?

Areas of personal growth? Areas that need improvement?

What are your goals next month in your time with the Lord?

Additional thoughts, reflections, and prayer:

REFLECT ON YOUR QUIET TIME THIS MONTH_____

_____Day 1	_____Day 11	_____Day 21
_____Day 2	_____Day 12	_____Day 22
_____Day 3	_____Day 13	_____Day 23
_____Day 4	_____Day 14	_____Day 24
_____Day 5	_____Day 15	_____Day 25
_____Day 6	_____Day 16	_____Day 26
_____Day 7	_____Day 17	_____Day 27
_____Day 8	_____Day 18	_____Day 28
_____Day 9	_____Day 19	_____Day 29
_____Day 10	_____Day 20	_____Day 30
		_____Day 31

What was the most significant insight from the Lord?

What was the most significant verse?

What was your favorite devotional reading?

What was the most significant answer to prayer?

Areas of personal growth? Areas that need improvement?

What are your goals next month in your time with the Lord?

Additional thoughts, reflections, and prayer:

REFLECT ON YOUR QUIET TIME THIS MONTH_____

_____Day 1	_____Day 11	_____Day 21
_____Day 2	_____Day 12	_____Day 22
_____Day 3	_____Day 13	_____Day 23
_____Day 4	_____Day 14	_____Day 24
_____Day 5	_____Day 15	_____Day 25
_____Day 6	_____Day 16	_____Day 26
_____Day 7	_____Day 17	_____Day 27
_____Day 8	_____Day 18	_____Day 28
_____Day 9	_____Day 19	_____Day 29
_____Day 10	_____Day 20	_____Day 30
		_____Day 31

What was the most significant insight from the Lord?

What was the most significant verse?

What was your favorite devotional reading?

What was the most significant answer to prayer?

Areas of personal growth? Areas that need improvement?

What are your goals next month in your time with the Lord?

Additional thoughts, reflections, and prayer:

REFLECT ON YOUR QUIET TIME THIS MONTH_____

_____Day 1	_____Day 11	_____Day 21
_____Day 2	_____Day 12	_____Day 22
_____Day 3	_____Day 13	_____Day 23
_____Day 4	_____Day 14	_____Day 24
_____Day 5	_____Day 15	_____Day 25
_____Day 6	_____Day 16	_____Day 26
_____Day 7	_____Day 17	_____Day 27
_____Day 8	_____Day 18	_____Day 28
_____Day 9	_____Day 19	_____Day 29
_____Day 10	_____Day 20	_____Day 30
		_____Day 31

What was the most significant insight from the Lord?

What was the most significant verse?

What was your favorite devotional reading?

What was the most significant answer to prayer?

Areas of personal growth? Areas that need improvement?

What are your goals next month in your time with the Lord?

Additional thoughts, reflections, and prayer:

REFLECT ON YOUR QUIET TIME THIS MONTH_____

_____Day 1	_____Day 11	_____Day 21
_____Day 2	_____Day 12	_____Day 22
_____Day 3	_____Day 13	_____Day 23
_____Day 4	_____Day 14	_____Day 24
_____Day 5	_____Day 15	_____Day 25
_____Day 6	_____Day 16	_____Day 26
_____Day 7	_____Day 17	_____Day 27
_____Day 8	_____Day 18	_____Day 28
_____Day 9	_____Day 19	_____Day 29
_____Day 10	_____Day 20	_____Day 30
		_____Day 31

What was the most significant insight from the Lord?

What was the most significant verse?

What was your favorite devotional reading?

What was the most significant answer to prayer?

Areas of personal growth? Areas that need improvement?

What are your goals next month in your time with the Lord?

Additional thoughts, reflections, and prayer:

REFLECT ON YOUR QUIET TIME THIS MONTH_____

_____Day 1	_____Day 11	_____Day 21
_____Day 2	_____Day 12	_____Day 22
_____Day 3	_____Day 13	_____Day 23
_____Day 4	_____Day 14	_____Day 24
_____Day 5	_____Day 15	_____Day 25
_____Day 6	_____Day 16	_____Day 26
_____Day 7	_____Day 17	_____Day 27
_____Day 8	_____Day 18	_____Day 28
_____Day 9	_____Day 19	_____Day 29
_____Day 10	_____Day 20	_____Day 30
		_____Day 31

What was the most significant insight from the Lord?

What was the most significant verse?

What was your favorite devotional reading?

What was the most significant answer to prayer?

Areas of personal growth? Areas that need improvement?

What are your goals next month in your time with the Lord?

Additional thoughts, reflections, and prayer:

REFLECT ON YOUR QUIET TIME THIS MONTH_____

_____Day 1	_____Day 11	_____Day 21
_____Day 2	_____Day 12	_____Day 22
_____Day 3	_____Day 13	_____Day 23
_____Day 4	_____Day 14	_____Day 24
_____Day 5	_____Day 15	_____Day 25
_____Day 6	_____Day 16	_____Day 26
_____Day 7	_____Day 17	_____Day 27
_____Day 8	_____Day 18	_____Day 28
_____Day 9	_____Day 19	_____Day 29
_____Day 10	_____Day 20	_____Day 30
		_____Day 31

What was the most significant insight from the Lord?

What was the most significant verse?

What was your favorite devotional reading?

What was the most significant answer to prayer?

Areas of personal growth? Areas that need improvement?

What are your goals next month in your time with the Lord?

Additional thoughts, reflections, and prayer:

REFLECT ON YOUR QUIET TIME THIS MONTH_____

_____Day 1	_____Day 11	_____Day 21
_____Day 2	_____Day 12	_____Day 22
_____Day 3	_____Day 13	_____Day 23
_____Day 4	_____Day 14	_____Day 24
_____Day 5	_____Day 15	_____Day 25
_____Day 6	_____Day 16	_____Day 26
_____Day 7	_____Day 17	_____Day 27
_____Day 8	_____Day 18	_____Day 28
_____Day 9	_____Day 19	_____Day 29
_____Day 10	_____Day 20	_____Day 30
		_____Day 31

What was the most significant insight from the Lord?

What was the most significant verse?

What was your favorite devotional reading?

What was the most significant answer to prayer?

Areas of personal growth? Areas that need improvement?

What are your goals next month in your time with the Lord?

Additional thoughts, reflections, and prayer:

REFLECT ON YOUR QUIET TIME THIS MONTH_____

_____Day 1	_____Day 11	_____Day 21
_____Day 2	_____Day 12	_____Day 22
_____Day 3	_____Day 13	_____Day 23
_____Day 4	_____Day 14	_____Day 24
_____Day 5	_____Day 15	_____Day 25
_____Day 6	_____Day 16	_____Day 26
_____Day 7	_____Day 17	_____Day 27
_____Day 8	_____Day 18	_____Day 28
_____Day 9	_____Day 19	_____Day 29
_____Day 10	_____Day 20	_____Day 30
		_____Day 31

What was the most significant insight from the Lord?

What was the most significant verse?

What was your favorite devotional reading?

What was the most significant answer to prayer?

Areas of personal growth? Areas that need improvement?

What are your goals next month in your time with the Lord?

Additional thoughts, reflections, and prayer:

REFLECT ON YOUR QUIET TIME THIS MONTH_____

_____Day 1	_____Day 11	_____Day 21
_____Day 2	_____Day 12	_____Day 22
_____Day 3	_____Day 13	_____Day 23
_____Day 4	_____Day 14	_____Day 24
_____Day 5	_____Day 15	_____Day 25
_____Day 6	_____Day 16	_____Day 26
_____Day 7	_____Day 17	_____Day 27
_____Day 8	_____Day 18	_____Day 28
_____Day 9	_____Day 19	_____Day 29
_____Day 10	_____Day 20	_____Day 30
		_____Day 31

What was the most significant insight from the Lord?

What was the most significant verse?

What was your favorite devotional reading?

What was the most significant answer to prayer?

Areas of personal growth? Areas that need improvement?

What are your goals next month in your time with the Lord?

Additional thoughts, reflections, and prayer:

REFLECT ON YOUR QUIET TIME THIS MONTH_____

_____Day 1	_____Day 11	_____Day 21
_____Day 2	_____Day 12	_____Day 22
_____Day 3	_____Day 13	_____Day 23
_____Day 4	_____Day 14	_____Day 24
_____Day 5	_____Day 15	_____Day 25
_____Day 6	_____Day 16	_____Day 26
_____Day 7	_____Day 17	_____Day 27
_____Day 8	_____Day 18	_____Day 28
_____Day 9	_____Day 19	_____Day 29
_____Day 10	_____Day 20	_____Day 30
		_____Day 31

What was the most significant insight from the Lord?

What was the most significant verse?

What was your favorite devotional reading?

What was the most significant answer to prayer?

Areas of personal growth? Areas that need improvement?

What are your goals next month in your time with the Lord?

Additional thoughts, reflections, and prayer:

REFLECT ON YOUR QUIET TIME THIS MONTH_____

_____Day 1	_____Day 11	_____Day 21
_____Day 2	_____Day 12	_____Day 22
_____Day 3	_____Day 13	_____Day 23
_____Day 4	_____Day 14	_____Day 24
_____Day 5	_____Day 15	_____Day 25
_____Day 6	_____Day 16	_____Day 26
_____Day 7	_____Day 17	_____Day 27
_____Day 8	_____Day 18	_____Day 28
_____Day 9	_____Day 19	_____Day 29
_____Day 10	_____Day 20	_____Day 30
		_____Day 31

What was the most significant insight from the Lord?

What was the most significant verse?

What was your favorite devotional reading?

What was the most significant answer to prayer?

Areas of personal growth? Areas that need improvement?

What are your goals next month in your time with the Lord?

Additional thoughts, reflections, and prayer:

THE FOCUS OF YOUR DEVOTION

Listen to my words, LORD, consider my lament. Hear my cry
for help, my King and my God, for to you I pray.
PSALM 5:1-2

PREPARE YOUR HEART

Two thousand years ago, the most extraordinary Person to ever walk the face of this earth lived and laughed and spent time with friends and family. His name is Jesus. His life and purpose is outlined in the Old and New Testaments of the Bible. And He lives today! If you could spend time with Jesus today, would you? Write a brief prayer asking the Lord to give you a new awareness of His presence and renew your passion for Him.

READ AND STUDY GOD'S WORD

1. Christian devotion is a solemn, passionate dedication and exclusive commitment to Jesus Christ in the power of the Holy Spirit. To be devoted to God implies commitment, loyalty, fidelity, respect, passion, and exclusive attachment. Psalm 5, written by David, speaks of his deep devotion to God. Read Psalm 5 and record what you notice about David's devotion.

2. What actions by David demonstrate his devotion to God?

3. Look at the following three events in the life of Jesus and describe the devotion that is apparent in each one.

Matthew 4:18-5:1

Matthew 14:22-36

Matthew 26:6-13

4. Why were people drawn to Jesus? What do you think it was about Him that caused them to follow Him wherever He went and listen to Him when He spoke? Look at the following verses for insight into these questions: Matthew 7:28-29, 9:35-36, 15:32, 23:37, John 15:9, 17:23.

ADORE GOD IN PRAYER

If Jesus were to walk into your room, what would you say to Him? Today imagine that you are sitting with Jesus. Though you cannot see Him with your physical eyes, He is with you even now. Talk to Him, knowing that He is right here with you. Pour out to Him all that is on your heart. You may wish to close your eyes to shut out the world and simply focus on your Lord.

YIELD YOURSELF TO GOD

Is it not unspeakably delightful to view the Savior in all His offices, and to perceive Him matchless in each—to shift the kaleidoscope, as it were, and to find fresh combinations of peerless graces? In the manger and in eternity, on the cross and on His throne, in the garden and in His kingdom, among thieves or in the midst of cherubim, He is everywhere "altogether lovely." Examine carefully every little act of His life, and every trait of His character, and He is as lovely in the minute as in the majestic. Judge Him as you will, you cannot censure; weigh Him as you please, and He will not be found wanting. Eternity shall not discover the shadow of a spot in our Beloved, but rather, as ages resolve, His hidden glories shall shine forth with yet more inconceivable splendor, and His unutterable loveliness shall more and more ravish all celestial minds.

CHARLES SPURGEON IN MORNING AND EVENING

ENJOY HIS PRESENCE

What have you learned about devotion to God today from David's example and the examples in the New Testament? How intimate is your own love relationship with your Lord? In what ways can you express devotion to your Lord today?

REST IN HIS LOVE

"He who loves me will be loved by my Father, and I too will love Him and show myself to him" (John 14:21).[1]

THE QUIET TIME
NOTEBOOK PAGES

JOURNAL

"Pour out your heart like water in the
presence of the Lord" — Lamentations 2:19 NIV

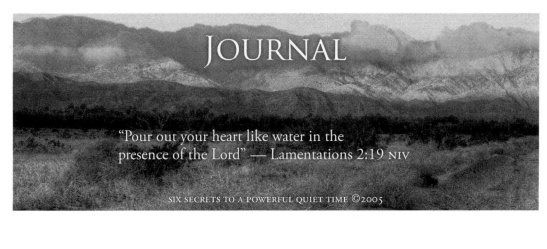

JOURNAL

"Pour out your heart like water in the presence of the Lord" — Lamentations 2:19 NIV

SIX SECRETS TO A POWERFUL QUIET TIME ©2005

....

....

....

....

....

....

....

....

....

....

....

....

....

....

JOURNAL

"Pour out your heart like water in the
presence of the Lord" — Lamentations 2:19 NIV

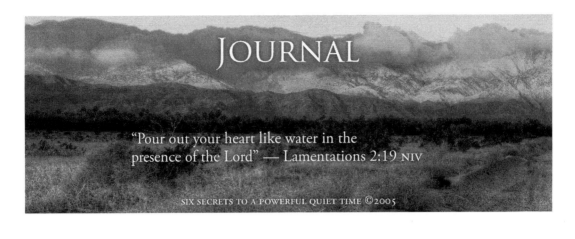

JOURNAL

"Pour out your heart like water in the
presence of the Lord" — Lamentations 2:19 NIV

SIX SECRETS TO A POWERFUL QUIET TIME ©2005

JOURNAL

"Pour out your heart like water in the
presence of the Lord" — Lamentations 2:19 NIV

....

....

....

....

....

....

....

....

....

....

....

....

....

....

....

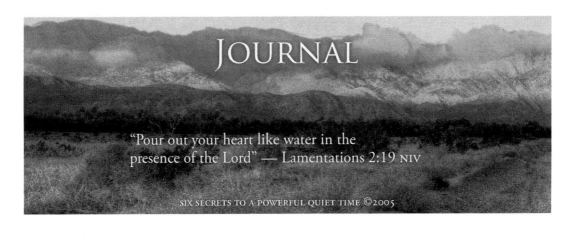

JOURNAL

"Pour out your heart like water in the presence of the Lord" — Lamentations 2:19 NIV

SIX SECRETS TO A POWERFUL QUIET TIME ©2005

JOURNAL

"Pour out your heart like water in the
presence of the Lord" — Lamentations 2:19 NIV

Journal

"Pour out your heart like water in the
presence of the Lord" — Lamentations 2:19 NIV

JOURNAL

"Pour out your heart like water in the
presence of the Lord" — Lamentations 2:19 NIV

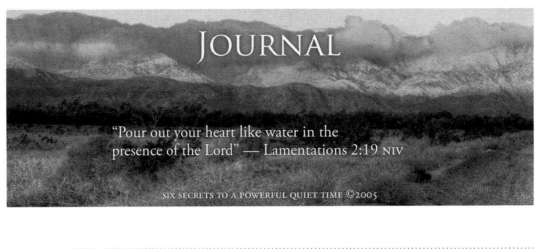

JOURNAL

"Pour out your heart like water in the presence of the Lord" — Lamentations 2:19 NIV

SIX SECRETS TO A POWERFUL QUIET TIME ©2005

....

....

....

....

....

....

....

....

....

....

....

....

....

....

....

JOURNAL

"Pour out your heart like water in the
presence of the Lord" — Lamentations 2:19 NIV

JOURNAL

"Pour out your heart like water in the
presence of the Lord" — Lamentations 2:19 NIV

Journal

"Pour out your heart like water in the presence of the Lord" — Lamentations 2:19 NIV

SIX SECRETS TO A POWERFUL QUIET TIME ©2005

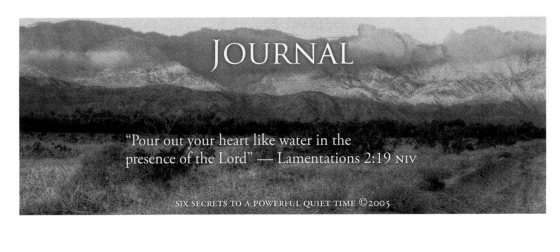

JOURNAL

"Pour out your heart like water in the
presence of the Lord" — Lamentations 2:19 NIV

Journal

"Pour out your heart like water in the
presence of the Lord" — Lamentations 2:19 NIV

JOURNAL

"Pour out your heart like water in the presence of the Lord" — Lamentations 2:19 NIV

Journal

"Pour out your heart like water in the presence of the Lord" — Lamentations 2:19 NIV

SIX SECRETS TO A POWERFUL QUIET TIME ©2005

....

....

....

....

....

....

....

....

....

....

....

....

....

....

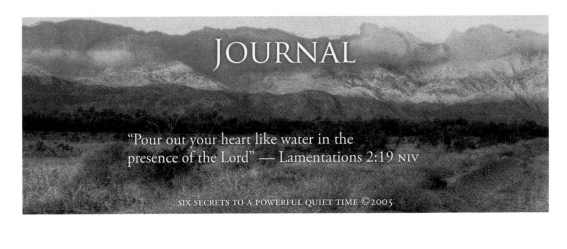

JOURNAL

"Pour out your heart like water in the
presence of the Lord" — Lamentations 2:19 NIV

SIX SECRETS TO A POWERFUL QUIET TIME ©2005

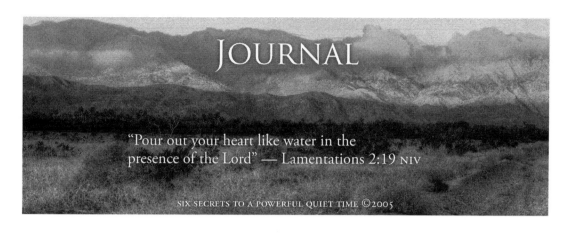

JOURNAL

"Pour out your heart like water in the
presence of the Lord" — Lamentations 2:19 NIV

SIX SECRETS TO A POWERFUL QUIET TIME ©2005

....

....

....

....

....

....

....

....

....

....

....

....

....

....

....

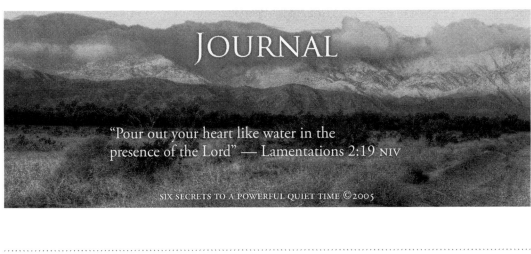

JOURNAL

"Pour out your heart like water in the
presence of the Lord" — Lamentations 2:19 NIV

JOURNAL

"Pour out your heart like water in the
presence of the Lord" — Lamentations 2:19 NIV

....

....

....

....

....

....

....

....

....

....

....

....

....

....

....

JOURNAL

"Pour out your heart like water in the
presence of the Lord" — Lamentations 2:19 NIV

JOURNAL

"Pour out your heart like water in the
presence of the Lord" — Lamentations 2:19 NIV

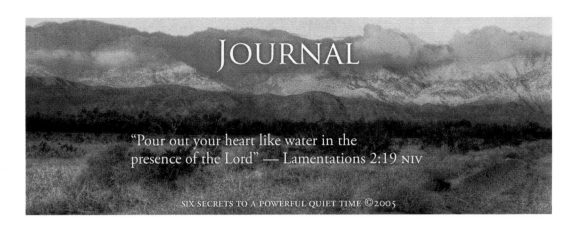

JOURNAL

"Pour out your heart like water in the presence of the Lord" — Lamentations 2:19 NIV

SIX SECRETS TO A POWERFUL QUIET TIME ©2005

JOURNAL

"Pour out your heart like water in the
presence of the Lord" — Lamentations 2:19 NIV

....

....

....

....

....

....

....

....

....

....

....

....

....

....

JOURNAL

"Pour out your heart like water in the
presence of the Lord" — Lamentations 2:19 NIV

JOURNAL

"Pour out your heart like water in the
presence of the Lord" — Lamentations 2:19 NIV

....

....

....

....

....

....

....

....

....

....

....

....

....

....

....

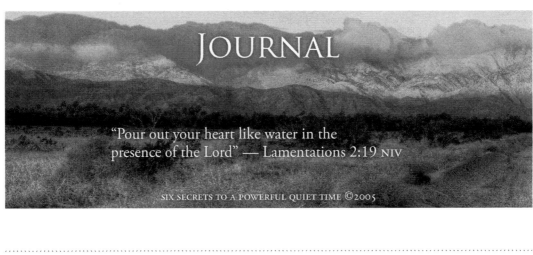

JOURNAL

"Pour out your heart like water in the presence of the Lord" — Lamentations 2:19 NIV

SIX SECRETS TO A POWERFUL QUIET TIME ©2005

JOURNAL

"Pour out your heart like water in the
presence of the Lord" — Lamentations 2:19 NIV

....

....

....

....

....

....

....

....

....

....

....

....

....

....

....

....

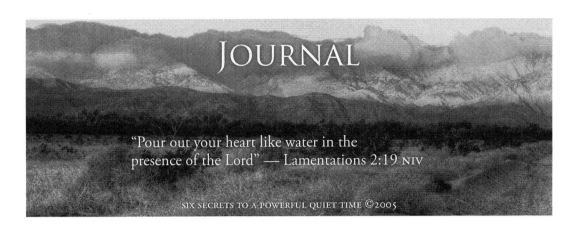

JOURNAL

"Pour out your heart like water in the
presence of the Lord" — Lamentations 2:19 NIV

SIX SECRETS TO A POWERFUL QUIET TIME ©2005

....

....

....

....

....

....

....

....

....

....

....

....

....

....

....

JOURNAL

"Pour out your heart like water in the
presence of the Lord" — Lamentations 2:19 NIV

SIX SECRETS TO A POWERFUL QUIET TIME ©2005

....

....

....

....

....

....

....

....

....

....

....

....

....

....

....

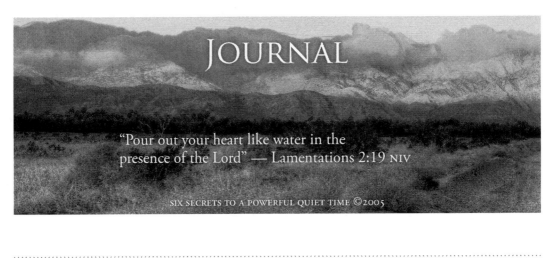

JOURNAL

"Pour out your heart like water in the presence of the Lord" — Lamentations 2:19 NIV

SIX SECRETS TO A POWERFUL QUIET TIME ©2005

....

....

....

....

....

....

....

....

....

....

....

....

....

....

....

....

JOURNAL

"Pour out your heart like water in the presence of the Lord" — Lamentations 2:19 NIV

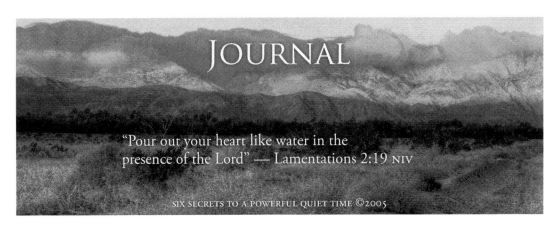

JOURNAL

"Pour out your heart like water in the
presence of the Lord" — Lamentations 2:19 NIV

SIX SECRETS TO A POWERFUL QUIET TIME ©2005

JOURNAL

"Pour out your heart like water in the
presence of the Lord" — Lamentations 2:19 NIV

....

....

....

....

....

....

....

....

....

....

....

....

....

....

....

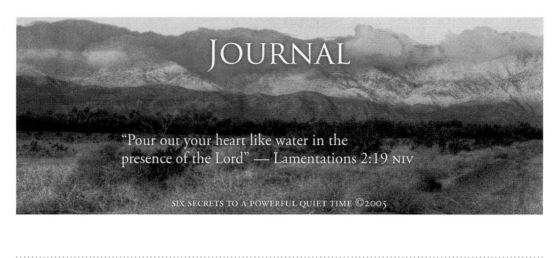

JOURNAL

"Pour out your heart like water in the presence of the Lord" — Lamentations 2:19 NIV

SIX SECRETS TO A POWERFUL QUIET TIME ©2005

....

....

....

....

....

....

....

....

....

....

....

....

....

....

....

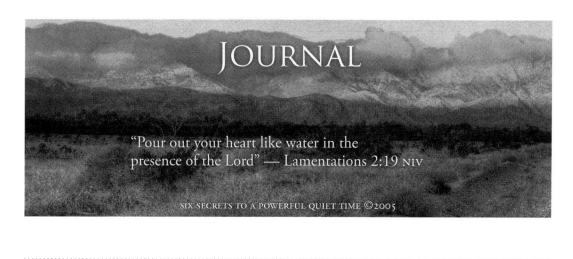

JOURNAL

"Pour out your heart like water in the presence of the Lord" — Lamentations 2:19 NIV

SIX SECRETS TO A POWERFUL QUIET TIME ©2005

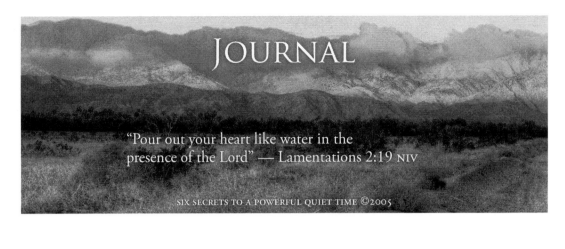

JOURNAL

"Pour out your heart like water in the
presence of the Lord" — Lamentations 2:19 NIV

SIX SECRETS TO A POWERFUL QUIET TIME ©2005

....

....

....

....

....

....

....

....

....

....

....

....

....

....

JOURNAL

"Pour out your heart like water in the
presence of the Lord" — Lamentations 2:19 NIV

SIX SECRETS TO A POWERFUL QUIET TIME ©2005

JOURNAL

"Pour out your heart like water in the
presence of the Lord" — Lamentations 2:19 NIV

....

....

....

....

....

....

....

....

....

....

....

....

....

....

JOURNAL

"Pour out your heart like water in the
presence of the Lord" — Lamentations 2:19 NIV

....

....

....

....

....

....

....

....

....

....

....

....

....

....

....

....

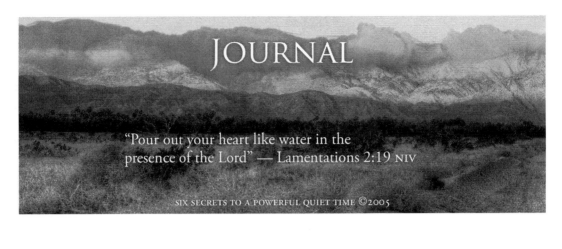

JOURNAL

"Pour out your heart like water in the
presence of the Lord" — Lamentations 2:19 NIV

SIX SECRETS TO A POWERFUL QUIET TIME ©2005

JOURNAL

"Pour out your heart like water in the presence of the Lord" — Lamentations 2:19 NIV

SIX SECRETS TO A POWERFUL QUIET TIME ©2005

....

....

....

....

....

....

....

....

....

....

....

....

....

....

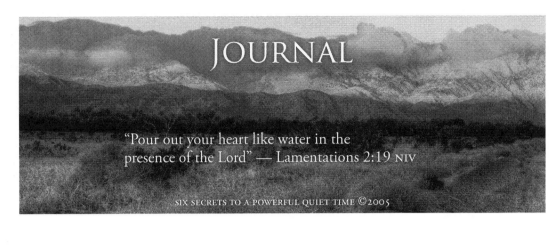

JOURNAL

"Pour out your heart like water in the presence of the Lord" — Lamentations 2:19 NIV

JOURNAL

"Pour out your heart like water in the
presence of the Lord" — Lamentations 2:19 NIV

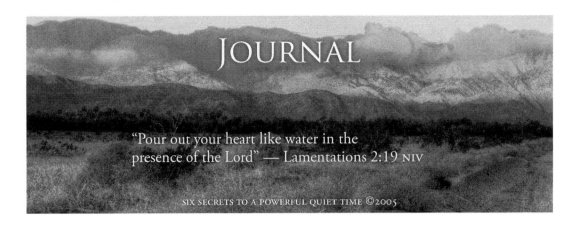

JOURNAL

"Pour out your heart like water in the
presence of the Lord" — Lamentations 2:19 NIV

SIX SECRETS TO A POWERFUL QUIET TIME ©2005

Journal

"Pour out your heart like water in the presence of the Lord" — Lamentations 2:19 NIV

SIX SECRETS TO A POWERFUL QUIET TIME ©2005

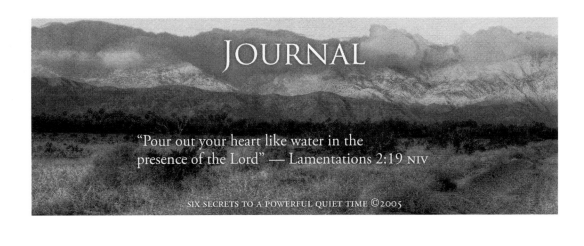

JOURNAL

"Pour out your heart like water in the presence of the Lord" — Lamentations 2:19 NIV

SIX SECRETS TO A POWERFUL QUIET TIME ©2005

JOURNAL

"Pour out your heart like water in the presence of the Lord" — Lamentations 2:19 NIV

....

....

....

....

....

....

....

....

....

....

....

....

....

....

....

JOURNAL

"Pour out your heart like water in the presence of the Lord" — Lamentations 2:19 NIV

JOURNAL

"Pour out your heart like water in the
presence of the Lord" — Lamentations 2:19 NIV

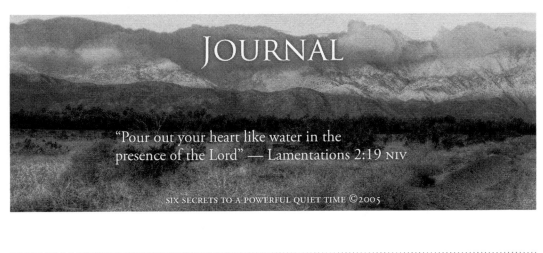

JOURNAL

"Pour out your heart like water in the presence of the Lord" — Lamentations 2:19 NIV

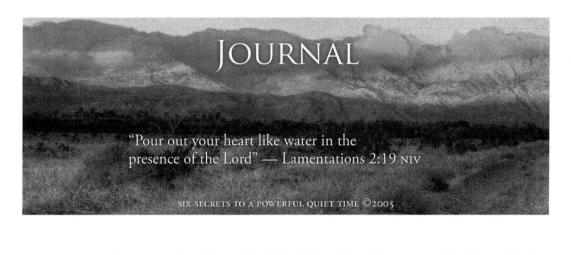

JOURNAL

"Pour out your heart like water in the presence of the Lord" — Lamentations 2:19 NIV

SIX SECRETS TO A POWERFUL QUIET TIME ©2005

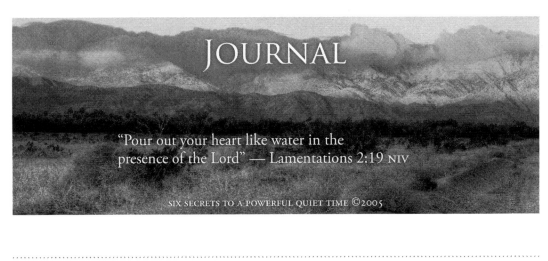

JOURNAL

"Pour out your heart like water in the
presence of the Lord" — Lamentations 2:19 NIV

SIX SECRETS TO A POWERFUL QUIET TIME ©2005

....

....

....

....

....

....

....

....

....

....

....

....

....

....

Journal

"Pour out your heart like water in the
presence of the Lord" — Lamentations 2:19 NIV

....

....

....

....

....

....

....

....

....

....

....

....

....

....

....

....

....

....

JOURNAL

"Pour out your heart like water in the
presence of the Lord" — Lamentations 2:19 NIV

JOURNAL

"Pour out your heart like water in the presence of the Lord" — Lamentations 2:19 NIV

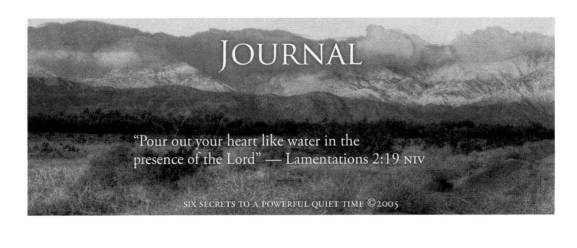

JOURNAL

"Pour out your heart like water in the presence of the Lord" — Lamentations 2:19 NIV

SIX SECRETS TO A POWERFUL QUIET TIME ©2005

JOURNAL

"Pour out your heart like water in the presence of the Lord" — Lamentations 2:19 NIV

SIX SECRETS TO A POWERFUL QUIET TIME ©2005

....

....

....

....

....

....

....

....

....

....

....

....

....

....

....

....

....

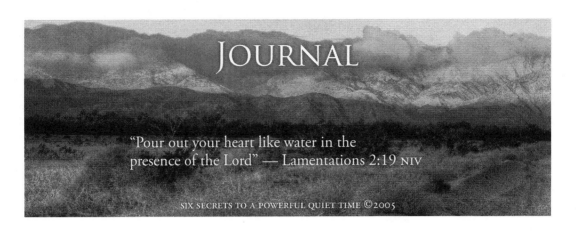

JOURNAL

"Pour out your heart like water in the
presence of the Lord" — Lamentations 2:19 NIV

....

....

....

....

....

....

....

....

....

....

....

....

....

....

....

....

READ & STUDY GOD'S WORD

"Study this book of the Law continually.
Meditate on it day and night..." — Joshua 1:8 NLT

SIX SECRETS TO A POWERFUL QUIET TIME ©2005

Date _____ Today's Scripture _____

Read God's Word — Record One Significant Observation

Immediate Context

Insights – Word Meanings – Cross-References

Summary & Conclusions

Application In My Life

READ & STUDY GOD'S WORD

"Study this book of the Law continually.
Meditate on it day and night..." — Joshua 1:8 NLT

SIX SECRETS TO A POWERFUL QUIET TIME ©2005

Date _____ Today's Scripture _____

Read God's Word — *Record One Significant Observation*

Immediate Context

Insights – Word Meanings – Cross-References

Summary & Conclusions

Application In My Life

READ & STUDY GOD'S WORD

"Study this book of the Law continually.
Meditate on it day and night..." — Joshua 1:8 NLT

SIX SECRETS TO A POWERFUL QUIET TIME ©2005

Date _____ Today's Scripture _____

Read God's Word — *Record One Significant Observation*

Immediate Context

Insights – Word Meanings – Cross-References

Summary & Conclusions

Application In My Life

READ & STUDY GOD'S WORD

"Study this book of the Law continually.
Meditate on it day and night..." — Joshua 1:8 NLT

SIX SECRETS TO A POWERFUL QUIET TIME ©2005

Date _____ Today's Scripture _____

Read God's Word — Record One Significant Observation

Immediate Context

Insights – Word Meanings – Cross-References

Summary & Conclusions

Application In My Life

READ & STUDY GOD'S WORD

"Study this book of the Law continually.
Meditate on it day and night..." — Joshua 1:8 NLT

SIX SECRETS TO A POWERFUL QUIET TIME ©2005

Date _____ Today's Scripture _____

Read God's Word — Record One Significant Observation

Immediate Context

Insights – Word Meanings – Cross-References

Summary & Conclusions

Application In My Life

READ & STUDY GOD'S WORD

"Study this book of the Law continually.
Meditate on it day and night..." — Joshua 1:8 NLT

SIX SECRETS TO A POWERFUL QUIET TIME ©2005

Date _____ Today's Scripture _____

Read God's Word — Record One Significant Observation

Immediate Context

Insights – Word Meanings – Cross-References

Summary & Conclusions

Application In My Life

READ & STUDY GOD'S WORD

"Study this book of the Law continually.
Meditate on it day and night..." — Joshua 1:8 NLT

SIX SECRETS TO A POWERFUL QUIET TIME ©2005

Date _____ Today's Scripture _____

Read God's Word — Record One Significant Observation

Immediate Context

Insights – Word Meanings – Cross-References

Summary & Conclusions

Application In My Life

READ & STUDY GOD'S WORD

"Study this book of the Law continually.
Meditate on it day and night..." — Joshua 1:8 NLT

SIX SECRETS TO A POWERFUL QUIET TIME ©2005

Date _____ Today's Scripture _____

Read God's Word — Record One Significant Observation

Immediate Context

Insights – Word Meanings – Cross-References

Summary & Conclusions

Application In My Life

READ & STUDY GOD'S WORD

"Study this book of the Law continually.
Meditate on it day and night..." — Joshua 1:8 NLT

Date _____ Today's Scripture _____

Read God's Word — Record One Significant Observation

Immediate Context

Insights – Word Meanings – Cross-References

Summary & Conclusions

Application In My Life

READ & STUDY GOD'S WORD

"Study this book of the Law continually.
Meditate on it day and night..." — Joshua 1:8 NLT

SIX SECRETS TO A POWERFUL QUIET TIME ©2005

Date _____ Today's Scripture _____

Read God's Word — Record One Significant Observation

Immediate Context

Insights – Word Meanings – Cross-References

Summary & Conclusions

Application In My Life

READ & STUDY GOD'S WORD

"Study this book of the Law continually.
Meditate on it day and night..." — Joshua 1:8 NLT

SIX SECRETS TO A POWERFUL QUIET TIME ©2005

Date _____ *Today's Scripture* _____

Read God's Word — Record One Significant Observation

Immediate Context

Insights – Word Meanings – Cross-References

Summary & Conclusions

Application In My Life

READ & STUDY GOD'S WORD

"Study this book of the Law continually.
Meditate on it day and night..." — Joshua 1:8 NLT

SIX SECRETS TO A POWERFUL QUIET TIME ©2005

Date _____ Today's Scripture _____

Read God's Word — Record One Significant Observation

Immediate Context

Insights – Word Meanings – Cross-References

Summary & Conclusions

Application In My Life

READ & STUDY GOD'S WORD

"Study this book of the Law continually.
Meditate on it day and night..." — Joshua 1:8 NLT

Date _____ Today's Scripture _____

Read God's Word — *Record One Significant Observation*

Immediate Context

Insights – Word Meanings – Cross-References

Summary & Conclusions

Application In My Life

READ & STUDY GOD'S WORD

"Study this book of the Law continually.
Meditate on it day and night..." — Joshua 1:8 NLT

SIX SECRETS TO A POWERFUL QUIET TIME ©2005

Date _____ Today's Scripture _____

Read God's Word — Record One Significant Observation

Immediate Context

Insights – Word Meanings – Cross-References

Summary & Conclusions

Application In My Life

READ & STUDY GOD'S WORD

"Study this book of the Law continually.
Meditate on it day and night..." — Joshua 1:8 NLT

Date _____ Today's Scripture _____

Read God's Word — Record One Significant Observation

Immediate Context

Insights – Word Meanings – Cross-References

Summary & Conclusions

Application In My Life

READ & STUDY GOD'S WORD

"Study this book of the Law continually.
Meditate on it day and night..." — Joshua 1:8 NLT

SIX SECRETS TO A POWERFUL QUIET TIME ©2005

Date _____ *Today's Scripture* _____

Read God's Word — Record One Significant Observation

Immediate Context

Insights – Word Meanings – Cross-References

Summary & Conclusions

Application In My Life

READ & STUDY GOD'S WORD

"Study this book of the Law continually.
Meditate on it day and night..." — Joshua 1:8 NLT

Date _____ Today's Scripture _____

Read God's Word — Record One Significant Observation

Immediate Context

Insights – Word Meanings – Cross-References

Summary & Conclusions

Application In My Life

READ & STUDY GOD'S WORD

"Study this book of the Law continually.
Meditate on it day and night..." — Joshua 1:8 NLT

SIX SECRETS TO A POWERFUL QUIET TIME ©2005

Date _____ Today's Scripture _____

Read God's Word — Record One Significant Observation

Immediate Context

Insights – Word Meanings – Cross-References

Summary & Conclusions

Application In My Life

READ & STUDY GOD'S WORD

"Study this book of the Law continually.
Meditate on it day and night..." — Joshua 1:8 NLT

SIX SECRETS TO A POWERFUL QUIET TIME ©2005

Date _____ Today's Scripture _____

Read God's Word — *Record One Significant Observation*

Immediate Context

Insights — Word Meanings — Cross-References

Summary & Conclusions

Application In My Life

READ & STUDY GOD'S WORD

"Study this book of the Law continually.
Meditate on it day and night..." — Joshua 1:8 NLT

SIX SECRETS TO A POWERFUL QUIET TIME ©2005

Date _____ Today's Scripture _____

Read God's Word — *Record One Significant Observation*

Immediate Context

Insights – *Word Meanings* – *Cross-References*

Summary & Conclusions

Application In My Life

READ & STUDY GOD'S WORD

"Study this book of the Law continually.
Meditate on it day and night..." — Joshua 1:8 NLT

SIX SECRETS TO A POWERFUL QUIET TIME ©2005

Date _____ Today's Scripture _____

Read God's Word — Record One Significant Observation

Immediate Context

Insights – Word Meanings – Cross-References

Summary & Conclusions

Application In My Life

READ & STUDY GOD'S WORD

"Study this book of the Law continually.
Meditate on it day and night..." — Joshua 1:8 NLT

SIX SECRETS TO A POWERFUL QUIET TIME ©2005

Date _____ Today's Scripture _____

Read God's Word — Record One Significant Observation

Immediate Context

Insights – Word Meanings – Cross-References

Summary & Conclusions

Application In My Life

READ & STUDY GOD'S WORD

"Study this book of the Law continually.
Meditate on it day and night..." — Joshua 1:8 NLT

SIX SECRETS TO A POWERFUL QUIET TIME ©2005

Date _____ Today's Scripture _____

Read God's Word — *Record One Significant Observation*

Immediate Context

Insights – Word Meanings – Cross-References

Summary & Conclusions

Application In My Life

READ & STUDY GOD'S WORD

"Study this book of the Law continually.
Meditate on it day and night..." — Joshua 1:8 NLT

SIX SECRETS TO A POWERFUL QUIET TIME ©2005

Date _____ Today's Scripture _____

Read God's Word — Record One Significant Observation

Immediate Context

Insights – Word Meanings – Cross-References

Summary & Conclusions

Application In My Life

READ & STUDY GOD'S WORD

"Study this book of the Law continually.
Meditate on it day and night..." — Joshua 1:8 NLT

SIX SECRETS TO A POWERFUL QUIET TIME ©2005

Date _____ Today's Scripture _____

Read God's Word — *Record One Significant Observation*

Immediate Context

Insights – Word Meanings – Cross-References

Summary & Conclusions

Application In My Life

READ & STUDY GOD'S WORD

"Study this book of the Law continually.
Meditate on it day and night..." — Joshua 1:8 NLT

SIX SECRETS TO A POWERFUL QUIET TIME ©2005

Date _____ Today's Scripture _____

Read God's Word — Record One Significant Observation

Immediate Context

Insights – Word Meanings – Cross-References

Summary & Conclusions

Application In My Life

READ & STUDY GOD'S WORD

"Study this book of the Law continually.
Meditate on it day and night..." — Joshua 1:8 NLT

SIX SECRETS TO A POWERFUL QUIET TIME ©2005

Date _____ Today's Scripture _____

Read God's Word — Record One Significant Observation

Immediate Context

Insights – Word Meanings – Cross-References

Summary & Conclusions

Application In My Life

READ & STUDY GOD'S WORD

"Study this book of the Law continually.
Meditate on it day and night..." — Joshua 1:8 NLT

Date _____ Today's Scripture _____

Read God's Word — Record One Significant Observation

Immediate Context

Insights – Word Meanings – Cross-References

Summary & Conclusions

Application In My Life

READ & STUDY GOD'S WORD

"Study this book of the Law continually.
Meditate on it day and night..." — Joshua 1:8 NLT

SIX SECRETS TO A POWERFUL QUIET TIME ©2005

Date _____ Today's Scripture _____

Read God's Word — Record One Significant Observation

Immediate Context

Insights – Word Meanings – Cross-References

Summary & Conclusions

Application In My Life

READ & STUDY GOD'S WORD

"Study this book of the Law continually.
Meditate on it day and night..." — Joshua 1:8 NLT

SIX SECRETS TO A POWERFUL QUIET TIME ©2005

Date _____ Today's Scripture _____

Read God's Word — Record One Significant Observation

Immediate Context

Insights – Word Meanings – Cross-References

Summary & Conclusions

Application In My Life

READ & STUDY GOD'S WORD

"Study this book of the Law continually.
Meditate on it day and night..." — Joshua 1:8 NLT

Date _____ Today's Scripture _____

Read God's Word — *Record One Significant Observation*

Immediate Context

Insights — Word Meanings — Cross-References

Summary & Conclusions

Application In My Life

READ & STUDY GOD'S WORD

"Study this book of the Law continually.
Meditate on it day and night..." — Joshua 1:8 NLT

SIX SECRETS TO A POWERFUL QUIET TIME ©2005

Date _____ *Today's Scripture* _____

Read God's Word — Record One Significant Observation

Immediate Context

Insights – Word Meanings – Cross-References

Summary & Conclusions

Application In My Life

READ & STUDY GOD'S WORD

"Study this book of the Law continually.
Meditate on it day and night..." — Joshua 1:8 NLT

SIX SECRETS TO A POWERFUL QUIET TIME ©2005

Date _____ Today's Scripture _____

Read God's Word — Record One Significant Observation

Immediate Context

Insights – Word Meanings – Cross-References

Summary & Conclusions

Application In My Life

READ & STUDY GOD'S WORD

"Study this book of the Law continually.
Meditate on it day and night..." — Joshua 1:8 NLT

SIX SECRETS TO A POWERFUL QUIET TIME ©2005

Date _____ Today's Scripture _____

Read God's Word — Record One Significant Observation

Immediate Context

Insights – Word Meanings – Cross-References

Summary & Conclusions

Application In My Life

READ & STUDY GOD'S WORD

"Study this book of the Law continually.
Meditate on it day and night..." — Joshua 1:8 NLT

Date _____ Today's Scripture _____

Read God's Word — Record One Significant Observation

Immediate Context

Insights – Word Meanings – Cross-References

Summary & Conclusions

Application In My Life

READ & STUDY GOD'S WORD

"Study this book of the Law continually.
Meditate on it day and night..." — Joshua 1:8 NLT

SIX SECRETS TO A POWERFUL QUIET TIME ©2005

Date _____ Today's Scripture _____

Read God's Word — Record One Significant Observation

Immediate Context

Insights – Word Meanings – Cross-References

Summary & Conclusions

Application In My Life

READ & STUDY GOD'S WORD

"Study this book of the Law continually.
Meditate on it day and night..." — Joshua 1:8 NLT

Date _____ Today's Scripture _____

Read God's Word — *Record One Significant Observation*

Immediate Context

Insights – Word Meanings – Cross-References

Summary & Conclusions

Application In My Life

READ & STUDY GOD'S WORD

"Study this book of the Law continually.
Meditate on it day and night..." — Joshua 1:8 NLT

SIX SECRETS TO A POWERFUL QUIET TIME ©2005

Date _____ Today's Scripture _____

Read God's Word — Record One Significant Observation

Immediate Context

Insights – Word Meanings – Cross-References

Summary & Conclusions

Application In My Life

READ & STUDY GOD'S WORD

"Study this book of the Law continually.
Meditate on it day and night..." — Joshua 1:8 NLT

SIX SECRETS TO A POWERFUL QUIET TIME ©2005

Date _____ *Today's Scripture* _____

Read God's Word — Record One Significant Observation

Immediate Context

Insights – Word Meanings – Cross-References

Summary & Conclusions

Application In My Life

READ & STUDY GOD'S WORD

"Study this book of the Law continually.
Meditate on it day and night..." — Joshua 1:8 NLT

SIX SECRETS TO A POWERFUL QUIET TIME ©2005

Date _____ Today's Scripture _____

Read God's Word — Record One Significant Observation

Immediate Context

Insights – Word Meanings – Cross-References

Summary & Conclusions

Application In My Life

READ & STUDY GOD'S WORD

"Study this book of the Law continually.
Meditate on it day and night..." — Joshua 1:8 NLT

SIX SECRETS TO A POWERFUL QUIET TIME ©2005

Date _____ Today's Scripture _____

Read God's Word — Record One Significant Observation

Immediate Context

Insights – Word Meanings – Cross-References

Summary & Conclusions

Application In My Life

READ & STUDY GOD'S WORD

"Study this book of the Law continually.
Meditate on it day and night..." — Joshua 1:8 NLT

SIX SECRETS TO A POWERFUL QUIET TIME ©2005

Date _____ Today's Scripture _____

Read God's Word — Record One Significant Observation

Immediate Context

Insights – Word Meanings – Cross-References

Summary & Conclusions

Application In My Life

READ & STUDY GOD'S WORD

"Study this book of the Law continually.
Meditate on it day and night..." — Joshua 1:8 NLT

SIX SECRETS TO A POWERFUL QUIET TIME ©2005

Date _____ Today's Scripture _____

Read God's Word — Record One Significant Observation

Immediate Context

Insights – Word Meanings – Cross-References

Summary & Conclusions

Application In My Life

READ & STUDY GOD'S WORD

"Study this book of the Law continually.
Meditate on it day and night..." — Joshua 1:8 NLT

SIX SECRETS TO A POWERFUL QUIET TIME ©2005

Date _____ Today's Scripture _____

Read God's Word — Record One Significant Observation

Immediate Context

Insights – Word Meanings – Cross-References

Summary & Conclusions

Application In My Life

READ & STUDY GOD'S WORD

"Study this book of the Law continually.
Meditate on it day and night..." — Joshua 1:8 NLT

SIX SECRETS TO A POWERFUL QUIET TIME ©2005

Date _____ Today's Scripture _____

Read God's Word — Record One Significant Observation

Immediate Context

Insights – Word Meanings – Cross-References

Summary & Conclusions

Application In My Life

READ & STUDY GOD'S WORD

"Study this book of the Law continually.
Meditate on it day and night..." — Joshua 1:8 NLT

SIX SECRETS TO A POWERFUL QUIET TIME ©2005

Date _____ Today's Scripture _____

Read God's Word — Record One Significant Observation

Immediate Context

Insights – Word Meanings – Cross-References

Summary & Conclusions

Application In My Life

READ & STUDY GOD'S WORD

"Study this book of the Law continually.
Meditate on it day and night…" — Joshua 1:8 NLT

SIX SECRETS TO A POWERFUL QUIET TIME ©2005

Date _____ Today's Scripture _____

Read God's Word — Record One Significant Observation

Immediate Context

Insights – Word Meanings – Cross-References

Summary & Conclusions

Application In My Life

READ & STUDY GOD'S WORD

"Study this book of the Law continually.
Meditate on it day and night..." — Joshua 1:8 NLT

SIX SECRETS TO A POWERFUL QUIET TIME ©2005

Date _____ Today's Scripture _____

Read God's Word — Record One Significant Observation

Immediate Context

Insights – Word Meanings – Cross-References

Summary & Conclusions

Application In My Life

READ & STUDY GOD'S WORD

"Study this book of the Law continually.
Meditate on it day and night..." — Joshua 1:8 NLT

SIX SECRETS TO A POWERFUL QUIET TIME ©2005

Date _____ Today's Scripture _____

Read God's Word — Record One Significant Observation

Immediate Context

Insights – Word Meanings – Cross-References

Summary & Conclusions

Application In My Life

READ & STUDY GOD'S WORD

"Study this book of the Law continually.
Meditate on it day and night..." — Joshua 1:8 NLT

SIX SECRETS TO A POWERFUL QUIET TIME ©2005

Date _____ Today's Scripture _____

Read God's Word — Record One Significant Observation

Immediate Context

Insights – Word Meanings – Cross-References

Summary & Conclusions

Application In My Life

READ & STUDY GOD'S WORD

"Study this book of the Law continually.
Meditate on it day and night..." — Joshua 1:8 NLT

Date _____ Today's Scripture _____

Read God's Word — Record One Significant Observation

Immediate Context

Insights – Word Meanings – Cross-References

Summary & Conclusions

Application In My Life

READ & STUDY GOD'S WORD

"Study this book of the Law continually.
Meditate on it day and night..." — Joshua 1:8 NLT

SIX SECRETS TO A POWERFUL QUIET TIME ©2005

Date _____ Today's Scripture _____

Read God's Word — Record One Significant Observation

Immediate Context

Insights – Word Meanings – Cross-References

Summary & Conclusions

Application In My Life

READ & STUDY GOD'S WORD

"Study this book of the Law continually.
Meditate on it day and night..." — Joshua 1:8 NLT

SIX SECRETS TO A POWERFUL QUIET TIME ©2005

Date _____ Today's Scripture _____

Read God's Word — Record One Significant Observation

Immediate Context

Insights – Word Meanings – Cross-References

Summary & Conclusions

Application In My Life

READ & STUDY GOD'S WORD

"Study this book of the Law continually.
Meditate on it day and night..." — Joshua 1:8 NLT

SIX SECRETS TO A POWERFUL QUIET TIME ©2005

Date _____ Today's Scripture _____

Read God's Word — Record One Significant Observation

Immediate Context

Insights – Word Meanings – Cross-References

Summary & Conclusions

Application In My Life

READ & STUDY GOD'S WORD

"Study this book of the Law continually.
Meditate on it day and night..." — Joshua 1:8 NLT

SIX SECRETS TO A POWERFUL QUIET TIME ©2005

Date _____ Today's Scripture _____

Read God's Word — Record One Significant Observation

Immediate Context

Insights – Word Meanings – Cross-References

Summary & Conclusions

Application In My Life

READ & STUDY GOD'S WORD

"Study this book of the Law continually.
Meditate on it day and night..." — Joshua 1:8 NLT

SIX SECRETS TO A POWERFUL QUIET TIME ©2005

Date _____ Today's Scripture _____

Read God's Word — Record One Significant Observation

Immediate Context

Insights – Word Meanings – Cross-References

Summary & Conclusions

Application In My Life

READ & STUDY GOD'S WORD

"Study this book of the Law continually.
Meditate on it day and night..." — Joshua 1:8 NLT

Date _____ Today's Scripture _____

Read God's Word — Record One Significant Observation

Immediate Context

Insights – Word Meanings – Cross-References

Summary & Conclusions

Application In My Life

READ & STUDY GOD'S WORD

"Study this book of the Law continually.
Meditate on it day and night..." — Joshua 1:8 NLT

SIX SECRETS TO A POWERFUL QUIET TIME ©2005

Date _____ Today's Scripture _____

Read God's Word — Record One Significant Observation

Immediate Context

Insights – Word Meanings – Cross-References

Summary & Conclusions

Application In My Life

READ & STUDY GOD'S WORD

"Study this book of the Law continually.
Meditate on it day and night..." — Joshua 1:8 NLT

SIX SECRETS TO A POWERFUL QUIET TIME ©2005

Date _____ Today's Scripture _____

Read God's Word — Record One Significant Observation

Immediate Context

Insights – Word Meanings – Cross-References

Summary & Conclusions

Application In My Life

READ & STUDY GOD'S WORD

"Study this book of the Law continually.
Meditate on it day and night..." — Joshua 1:8 NLT

SIX SECRETS TO A POWERFUL QUIET TIME ©2005

Date _____ Today's Scripture _____

Read God's Word — Record One Significant Observation

Immediate Context

Insights – Word Meanings – Cross-References

Summary & Conclusions

Application In My Life

ADORE GOD IN PRAYER

"Don't worry about anything;
instead, pray about everything" — Philippians 4:6 NIV

*Prayer for*_____

Date: Topic:

Scripture:

Request:

Answer:

Date: Topic:

Scripture:

Request:

Answer:

Date: Topic:

Scripture:

Request:

Answer:

Date: Topic:

Scripture:

Request:

Answer:

Date: Topic:

Scripture:

Request:

Answer:

ADORE GOD IN PRAYER

"Don't worry about anything; instead, pray about everything" — Philippians 4:6 NIV

Prayer for _____

Date: Topic:
Scripture:
Request:

Answer:

_____

Date: Topic:
Scripture:
Request:

Answer:

_____

Date: Topic:
Scripture:
Request:

Answer:

_____

Date: Topic:
Scripture:
Request:

Answer:

_____

Date: Topic:
Scripture:
Request:

Answer:

_____

ADORE GOD IN PRAYER

"Don't worry about anything;
instead, pray about everything" — Philippians 4:6 NIV

SIX SECRETS TO A POWERFUL QUIET TIME ©2005

*Prayer for*_____

Date: Topic:
Scripture:
Request:

Answer:

_____

Date: Topic:
Scripture:
Request:

Answer:

_____

Date: Topic:
Scripture:
Request:

Answer:

_____

Date: Topic:
Scripture:
Request:

Answer:

_____

Date: Topic:
Scripture:
Request:

Answer:

_____

ADORE GOD IN PRAYER

"Don't worry about anything;
instead, pray about everything" — Philippians 4:6 NIV

SIX SECRETS TO A POWERFUL QUIET TIME ©2005

*Prayer for*_____

Date: Topic:

Scripture:

Request:

Answer:

Date: Topic:

Scripture:

Request:

Answer:

Date: Topic:

Scripture:

Request:

Answer:

Date: Topic:

Scripture:

Request:

Answer:

Date: Topic:

Scripture:

Request:

Answer:

ADORE GOD IN PRAYER

"Don't worry about anything; instead, pray about everything" — Philippians 4:6 NIV

SIX SECRETS TO A POWERFUL QUIET TIME ©2005

Prayer for _____

Date: Topic:
Scripture:
Request:

Answer:

Date: Topic:
Scripture:
Request:

Answer:

Date: Topic:
Scripture:
Request:

Answer:

Date: Topic:
Scripture:
Request:

Answer:

Date: Topic:
Scripture:
Request:

Answer:

ADORE GOD IN PRAYER

"Don't worry about anything;
instead, pray about everything" — Philippians 4:6 NIV

SIX SECRETS TO A POWERFUL QUIET TIME ©2005

*Prayer for*_____

Date: Topic:
Scripture:
Request:

Answer:

Date: Topic:
Scripture:
Request:

Answer:

Date: Topic:
Scripture:
Request:

Answer:

Date: Topic:
Scripture:
Request:

Answer:

Date: Topic:
Scripture:
Request:

Answer:

ADORE GOD IN PRAYER

"Don't worry about anything;
instead, pray about everything" — Philippians 4:6 NIV

*Prayer for*_____

Date: Topic:

Scripture:

Request:

Answer:

Date: Topic:

Scripture:

Request:

Answer:

Date: Topic:

Scripture:

Request:

Answer:

Date: Topic:

Scripture:

Request:

Answer:

Date: Topic:

Scripture:

Request:

Answer:

ADORE GOD IN PRAYER

*"Don't worry about anything;
instead, pray about everything"* — Philippians 4:6 NIV

SIX SECRETS TO A POWERFUL QUIET TIME © 2005

*Prayer for*_____

Date: Topic:
Scripture:
Request:

Answer:

_____

Date: Topic:
Scripture:
Request:

Answer:

_____

Date: Topic:
Scripture:
Request:

Answer:

_____

Date: Topic:
Scripture:
Request:

Answer:

_____

Date: Topic:
Scripture:
Request:

Answer:

_____

ADORE GOD IN PRAYER

"Don't worry about anything;
instead, pray about everything" — Philippians 4:6 NIV

SIX SECRETS TO A POWERFUL QUIET TIME ©2005

Prayer for_____

Date: Topic:
Scripture:
Request:

Answer:

Date: Topic:
Scripture:
Request:

Answer:

Date: Topic:
Scripture:
Request:

Answer:

Date: Topic:
Scripture:
Request:

Answer:

Date: Topic:
Scripture:
Request:

Answer:

ADORE GOD IN PRAYER

"Don't worry about anything;
instead, pray about everything" — Philippians 4:6 NIV

SIX SECRETS TO A POWERFUL QUIET TIME © 2005

*Prayer for*_____

Date: Topic:
Scripture:
Request:

Answer:

Date: Topic:
Scripture:
Request:

Answer:

Date: Topic:
Scripture:
Request:

Answer:

Date: Topic:
Scripture:
Request:

Answer:

Date: Topic:
Scripture:
Request:

Answer:

ADORE GOD IN PRAYER

"Don't worry about anything;
instead, pray about everything" — Philippians 4:6 NIV

SIX SECRETS TO A POWERFUL QUIET TIME ©2005

*Prayer for*_____

Date: Topic:
Scripture:
Request:

Answer:

_____

Date: Topic:
Scripture:
Request:

Answer:

_____

Date: Topic:
Scripture:
Request:

Answer:

_____

Date: Topic:
Scripture:
Request:

Answer:

_____

Date: Topic:
Scripture:
Request:

Answer:

_____

ADORE GOD IN PRAYER

"Don't worry about anything;
instead, pray about everything" — Philippians 4:6 NIV

*Prayer for*_____

Date: Topic:
Scripture:
Request:

Answer:

_____

Date: Topic:
Scripture:
Request:

Answer:

_____

Date: Topic:
Scripture:
Request:

Answer:

_____

Date: Topic:
Scripture:
Request:

Answer:

_____

Date: Topic:
Scripture:
Request:

Answer:

_____

ADORE GOD IN PRAYER

"Don't worry about anything;
instead, pray about everything" — Philippians 4:6 NIV

Prayer for _____

Date: Topic:

Scripture:

Request:

Answer:

Date: Topic:

Scripture:

Request:

Answer:

Date: Topic:

Scripture:

Request:

Answer:

Date: Topic:

Scripture:

Request:

Answer:

Date: Topic:

Scripture:

Request:

Answer:

ADORE GOD IN PRAYER

"Don't worry about anything;
instead, pray about everything" — Philippians 4:6 NIV

*Prayer for*_____

Date: Topic:
Scripture:
Request:

Answer:

_____

Date: Topic:
Scripture:
Request:

Answer:

_____

Date: Topic:
Scripture:
Request:

Answer:

_____

Date: Topic:
Scripture:
Request:

Answer:

_____

Date: Topic:
Scripture:
Request:

Answer:

_____

ADORE GOD IN PRAYER

"Don't worry about anything;
instead, pray about everything" — Philippians 4:6 NIV

*Prayer for*_____

Date: Topic:
Scripture:
Request:

Answer:

_____

Date: Topic:
Scripture:
Request:

Answer:

_____

Date: Topic:
Scripture:
Request:

Answer:

_____

Date: Topic:
Scripture:
Request:

Answer:

_____

Date: Topic:
Scripture:
Request:

Answer:

_____

ADORE GOD IN PRAYER

"Don't worry about anything;
instead, pray about everything" — Philippians 4:6 NIV

SIX SECRETS TO A POWERFUL QUIET TIME ©2005

*Prayer for*_____

Date: Topic:

Scripture:

Request:

Answer:

_____

Date: Topic:

Scripture:

Request:

Answer:

_____

Date: Topic:

Scripture:

Request:

Answer:

_____

Date: Topic:

Scripture:

Request:

Answer:

_____

Date: Topic:

Scripture:

Request:

Answer:

_____

ADORE GOD IN PRAYER

"Don't worry about anything;
instead, pray about everything" — Philippians 4:6 NIV

SIX SECRETS TO A POWERFUL QUIET TIME ©2005

*Prayer for*_____

Date: Topic:

Scripture:

Request:

Answer:

Date: Topic:

Scripture:

Request:

Answer:

Date: Topic:

Scripture:

Request:

Answer:

Date: Topic:

Scripture:

Request:

Answer:

Date: Topic:

Scripture:

Request:

Answer:

ADORE GOD IN PRAYER

"Don't worry about anything;
instead, pray about everything" — Philippians 4:6 NIV

SIX SECRETS TO A POWERFUL QUIET TIME © 2005

*Prayer for*_____

Date: Topic:
Scripture:
Request:

Answer:

_____

Date: Topic:
Scripture:
Request:

Answer:

_____

Date: Topic:
Scripture:
Request:

Answer:

_____

Date: Topic:
Scripture:
Request:

Answer:

_____

Date: Topic:
Scripture:
Request:

Answer:

_____

ADORE GOD IN PRAYER

"Don't worry about anything;
instead, pray about everything" — Philippians 4:6 NIV

SIX SECRETS TO A POWERFUL QUIET TIME ©2005

*Prayer for*_____

Date: Topic:
Scripture:
Request:

Answer:

_____

Date: Topic:
Scripture:
Request:

Answer:

_____

Date: Topic:
Scripture:
Request:

Answer:

_____

Date: Topic:
Scripture:
Request:

Answer:

_____

Date: Topic:
Scripture:
Request:

Answer:

_____

ADORE GOD IN PRAYER

"Don't worry about anything;
instead, pray about everything" — Philippians 4:6 NIV

SIX SECRETS TO A POWERFUL QUIET TIME © 2005

*Prayer for*_____

Date: Topic:
Scripture:
Request:

Answer:

___

Date: Topic:
Scripture:
Request:

Answer:

___

Date: Topic:
Scripture:
Request:

Answer:

___

Date: Topic:
Scripture:
Request:

Answer:

___

Date: Topic:
Scripture:
Request:

Answer:

___

Adore God In Prayer

"Don't worry about anything;
instead, pray about everything" — Philippians 4:6 NIV

SIX SECRETS TO A POWERFUL QUIET TIME ©2005

*Prayer for*_____

Date: Topic:

Scripture:

Request:

Answer:

_____

Date: Topic:

Scripture:

Request:

Answer:

_____

Date: Topic:

Scripture:

Request:

Answer:

_____

Date: Topic:

Scripture:

Request:

Answer:

_____

Date: Topic:

Scripture:

Request:

Answer:

_____

ADORE GOD IN PRAYER

"Don't worry about anything;
instead, pray about everything" — Philippians 4:6 NIV

SIX SECRETS TO A POWERFUL QUIET TIME ©2005

*Prayer for*_____

Date: Topic:
Scripture:
Request:

Answer:

_____

Date: Topic:
Scripture:
Request:

Answer:

_____

Date: Topic:
Scripture:
Request:

Answer:

_____

Date: Topic:
Scripture:
Request:

Answer:

_____

Date: Topic:
Scripture:
Request:

Answer:

_____

ADORE GOD IN PRAYER

"Don't worry about anything;
instead, pray about everything" — Philippians 4:6 NIV

SIX SECRETS TO A POWERFUL QUIET TIME ©2005

*Prayer for*_____

Date: Topic:
Scripture:
Request:

Answer:

_____

Date: Topic:
Scripture:
Request:

Answer:

_____

Date: Topic:
Scripture:
Request:

Answer:

_____

Date: Topic:
Scripture:
Request:

Answer:

_____

Date: Topic:
Scripture:
Request:

Answer:

_____

ADORE GOD IN PRAYER

"Don't worry about anything;
instead, pray about everything" — Philippians 4:6 NIV

*Prayer for*_____

Date: Topic:
Scripture:
Request:

Answer:

_____

Date: Topic:
Scripture:
Request:

Answer:

_____

Date: Topic:
Scripture:
Request:

Answer:

_____

Date: Topic:
Scripture:
Request:

Answer:

_____

Date: Topic:
Scripture:
Request:

Answer:

_____

ADORE GOD IN PRAYER

"Don't worry about anything;
instead, pray about everything" — Philippians 4:6 NIV

SIX SECRETS TO A POWERFUL QUIET TIME ©2005

Prayer for _____

Date: Topic:
Scripture:
Request:

Answer:

Date: Topic:
Scripture:
Request:

Answer:

Date: Topic:
Scripture:
Request:

Answer:

Date: Topic:
Scripture:
Request:

Answer:

Date: Topic:
Scripture:
Request:

Answer:

ADORE GOD IN PRAYER

"Don't worry about anything;
instead, pray about everything" — Philippians 4:6 NIV

SIX SECRETS TO A POWERFUL QUIET TIME ©2005

Prayer for _____

Date: Topic:

Scripture:

Request:

Answer:

Date: Topic:

Scripture:

Request:

Answer:

Date: Topic:

Scripture:

Request:

Answer:

Date: Topic:

Scripture:

Request:

Answer:

Date: Topic:

Scripture:

Request:

Answer:

ADORE GOD IN PRAYER

"Don't worry about anything;
instead, pray about everything" — Philippians 4:6 NIV

SIX SECRETS TO A POWERFUL QUIET TIME ©2005

*Prayer for*_____

Date: Topic:
Scripture:
Request:

Answer:

Date: Topic:
Scripture:
Request:

Answer:

Date: Topic:
Scripture:
Request:

Answer:

Date: Topic:
Scripture:
Request:

Answer:

Date: Topic:
Scripture:
Request:

Answer:

ADORE GOD IN PRAYER

"Don't worry about anything;
instead, pray about everything" — Philippians 4:6 NIV

SIX SECRETS TO A POWERFUL QUIET TIME © 2005

*Prayer for*_____

Date: Topic:
Scripture:
Request:

Answer:

_____

Date: Topic:
Scripture:
Request:

Answer:

_____

Date: Topic:
Scripture:
Request:

Answer:

_____

Date: Topic:
Scripture:
Request:

Answer:

_____

Date: Topic:
Scripture:
Request:

Answer:

_____

ADORE GOD IN PRAYER

"Don't worry about anything;
instead, pray about everything" — Philippians 4:6 NIV

SIX SECRETS TO A POWERFUL QUIET TIME ©2005

*Prayer for*_____

Date: Topic:

Scripture:

Request:

Answer:

_____

Date: Topic:

Scripture:

Request:

Answer:

_____

Date: Topic:

Scripture:

Request:

Answer:

_____

Date: Topic:

Scripture:

Request:

Answer:

_____

Date: Topic:

Scripture:

Request:

Answer:

_____

ADORE GOD IN PRAYER

"Don't worry about anything;
instead, pray about everything" — Philippians 4:6 NIV

SIX SECRETS TO A POWERFUL QUIET TIME ©2005

*Prayer for*_____

Date: Topic:
Scripture:
Request:

Answer:

_____

Date: Topic:
Scripture:
Request:

Answer:

_____

Date: Topic:
Scripture:
Request:

Answer:

_____

Date: Topic:
Scripture:
Request:

Answer:

_____

Date: Topic:
Scripture:
Request:

Answer:

_____

ADORE GOD IN PRAYER

"Don't worry about anything; instead, pray about everything" — Philippians 4:6 NIV

Prayer for _____

Date: Topic:

Scripture:

Request:

Answer:

Date: Topic:

Scripture:

Request:

Answer:

Date: Topic:

Scripture:

Request:

Answer:

Date: Topic:

Scripture:

Request:

Answer:

Date: Topic:

Scripture:

Request:

Answer:

ADORE GOD IN PRAYER

"Don't worry about anything;
instead, pray about everything" — Philippians 4:6 NIV

SIX SECRETS TO A POWERFUL QUIET TIME © 2005

*Prayer for*_____

Date: Topic:
Scripture:
Request:

Answer:
_____

Date: Topic:
Scripture:
Request:

Answer:
_____

Date: Topic:
Scripture:
Request:

Answer:
_____

Date: Topic:
Scripture:
Request:

Answer:
_____

Date: Topic:
Scripture:
Request:

Answer:
_____

Adore God In Prayer

"Don't worry about anything;
instead, pray about everything" — Philippians 4:6 NIV

SIX SECRETS TO A POWERFUL QUIET TIME ©2005

Prayer for _____

Date: Topic:

Scripture:

Request:

Answer:

Date: Topic:

Scripture:

Request:

Answer:

Date: Topic:

Scripture:

Request:

Answer:

Date: Topic:

Scripture:

Request:

Answer:

Date: Topic:

Scripture:

Request:

Answer:

ADORE GOD IN PRAYER

"Don't worry about anything;
instead, pray about everything" — Philippians 4:6 NIV

SIX SECRETS TO A POWERFUL QUIET TIME ©2005

*Prayer for*_____

Date: Topic:
Scripture:
Request:

Answer:

_____

Date: Topic:
Scripture:
Request:

Answer:

_____

Date: Topic:
Scripture:
Request:

Answer:

_____

Date: Topic:
Scripture:
Request:

Answer:

_____

Date: Topic:
Scripture:
Request:

Answer:

_____

ADORE GOD IN PRAYER

"Don't worry about anything;
instead, pray about everything" — Philippians 4:6 NIV

SIX SECRETS TO A POWERFUL QUIET TIME. ©2005

*Prayer for*_____

Date: Topic:

Scripture:

Request:

Answer:

Date: Topic:

Scripture:

Request:

Answer:

Date: Topic:

Scripture:

Request:

Answer:

Date: Topic:

Scripture:

Request:

Answer:

Date: Topic:

Scripture:

Request:

Answer:

ADORE GOD IN PRAYER

*"Don't worry about anything;
instead, pray about everything"* — Philippians 4:6 NIV

SIX SECRETS TO A POWERFUL QUIET TIME ©2005

Prayer for _____

Date: Topic:

Scripture:

Request:

Answer:

Date: Topic:

Scripture:

Request:

Answer:

Date: Topic:

Scripture:

Request:

Answer:

Date: Topic:

Scripture:

Request:

Answer:

Date: Topic:

Scripture:

Request:

Answer:

ADORE GOD IN PRAYER

"Don't worry about anything; instead, pray about everything" — Philippians 4:6 NIV

SIX SECRETS TO A POWERFUL QUIET TIME ©2005

*Prayer for*_____

Date: Topic:
Scripture:
Request:

Answer:
_____

Date: Topic:
Scripture:
Request:

Answer:
_____

Date: Topic:
Scripture:
Request:

Answer:
_____

Date: Topic:
Scripture:
Request:

Answer:
_____

Date: Topic:
Scripture:
Request:

Answer:
_____

ADORE GOD IN PRAYER

"Don't worry about anything;
instead, pray about everything" — Philippians 4:6 NIV

SIX SECRETS TO A POWERFUL QUIET TIME ©2005

*Prayer for*_____

Date: Topic:
Scripture:
Request:

Answer:

_____

Date: Topic:
Scripture:
Request:

Answer:

_____

Date: Topic:
Scripture:
Request:

Answer:

_____

Date: Topic:
Scripture:
Request:

Answer:

_____

Date: Topic:
Scripture:
Request:

Answer:

_____

ADORE GOD IN PRAYER

"Don't worry about anything;
instead, pray about everything" — Philippians 4:6 NIV

SIX SECRETS TO A POWERFUL QUIET TIME ©2005

*Prayer for*_____

Date: Topic:
Scripture:
Request:

Answer:

Date: Topic:
Scripture:
Request:

Answer:

Date: Topic:
Scripture:
Request:

Answer:

Date: Topic:
Scripture:
Request:

Answer:

Date: Topic:
Scripture:
Request:

Answer:

ADORE GOD IN PRAYER

"Don't worry about anything;
instead, pray about everything" — Philippians 4:6 NIV

SIX SECRETS TO A POWERFUL QUIET TIME ©2005

*Prayer for*_____

Date: Topic:
Scripture:
Request:

Answer:

_____

Date: Topic:
Scripture:
Request:

Answer:

_____

Date: Topic:
Scripture:
Request:

Answer:

_____

Date: Topic:
Scripture:
Request:

Answer:

_____

Date: Topic:
Scripture:
Request:

Answer:

_____

ADORE GOD IN PRAYER

"Don't worry about anything;
instead, pray about everything" — Philippians 4:6 NIV

SIX SECRETS TO A POWERFUL QUIET TIME ©2005

*Prayer for*_____

Date: Topic:

Scripture:

Request:

Answer:

_____

Date: Topic:

Scripture:

Request:

Answer:

_____

Date: Topic:

Scripture:

Request:

Answer:

_____

Date: Topic:

Scripture:

Request:

Answer:

_____

Date: Topic:

Scripture:

Request:

Answer:

_____

ADORE GOD IN PRAYER

"Don't worry about anything; instead, pray about everything" — Philippians 4:6 NIV

SIX SECRETS TO A POWERFUL QUIET TIME ©2005

Prayer for _____

Date: Topic:
Scripture:
Request:

Answer:

_____

Date: Topic:
Scripture:
Request:

Answer:

_____

Date: Topic:
Scripture:
Request:

Answer:

_____

Date: Topic:
Scripture:
Request:

Answer:

_____

Date: Topic:
Scripture:
Request:

Answer:

_____

ADORE GOD IN PRAYER

"Don't worry about anything;
instead, pray about everything" — Philippians 4:6 NIV

*Prayer for*_____

Date: Topic:

Scripture:

Request:

Answer:

_____

Date: Topic:

Scripture:

Request:

Answer:

_____

Date: Topic:

Scripture:

Request:

Answer:

_____

Date: Topic:

Scripture:

Request:

Answer:

_____

Date: Topic:

Scripture:

Request:

Answer:

_____

ADORE GOD IN PRAYER

"Don't worry about anything;
instead, pray about everything" — Philippians 4:6 NIV

SIX SECRETS TO A POWERFUL QUIET TIME ©2005

*Prayer for*_____

Date: Topic:

Scripture:

Request:

Answer:

Date: Topic:

Scripture:

Request:

Answer:

Date: Topic:

Scripture:

Request:

Answer:

Date: Topic:

Scripture:

Request:

Answer:

Date: Topic:

Scripture:

Request:

Answer:

Adore God In Prayer

"Don't worry about anything;
instead, pray about everything" — Philippians 4:6 NIV

SIX SECRETS TO A POWERFUL QUIET TIME ©2005

*Prayer for*_____

Date: Topic:
Scripture:
Request:

Answer:
_____

Date: Topic:
Scripture:
Request:

Answer:
_____

Date: Topic:
Scripture:
Request:

Answer:
_____

Date: Topic:
Scripture:
Request:

Answer:
_____

Date: Topic:
Scripture:
Request:

Answer:
_____

*Prayer for*_____

Date: Topic:
Scripture:
Request:

Answer:

_____

Date: Topic:
Scripture:
Request:

Answer:

_____

Date: Topic:
Scripture:
Request:

Answer:

_____

Date: Topic:
Scripture:
Request:

Answer:

_____

Date: Topic:
Scripture:
Request:

Answer:

_____

ADORE GOD IN PRAYER

"Don't worry about anything; instead, pray about everything" — Philippians 4:6 NIV

*Prayer for*_____

Date: Topic:

Scripture:

Request:

Answer:

_____

Date: Topic:

Scripture:

Request:

Answer:

_____

Date: Topic:

Scripture:

Request:

Answer:

_____

Date: Topic:

Scripture:

Request:

Answer:

_____

Date: Topic:

Scripture:

Request:

Answer:

_____

ADORE GOD IN PRAYER

"Don't worry about anything;
instead, pray about everything" — Philippians 4:6 NIV

SIX SECRETS TO A POWERFUL QUIET TIME ©2005

*Prayer for*_____

Date: Topic:
Scripture:
Request:

Answer:

Date: Topic:
Scripture:
Request:

Answer:

Date: Topic:
Scripture:
Request:

Answer:

Date: Topic:
Scripture:
Request:

Answer:

Date: Topic:
Scripture:
Request:

Answer:

ADORE GOD IN PRAYER

"Don't worry about anything;
instead, pray about everything" — Philippians 4:6 NIV

SIX SECRETS TO A POWERFUL QUIET TIME ©2005

*Prayer for*_____

Date: Topic:

Scripture:

Request:

Answer:

_____

Date: Topic:

Scripture:

Request:

Answer:

_____

Date: Topic:

Scripture:

Request:

Answer:

_____

Date: Topic:

Scripture:

Request:

Answer:

_____

Date: Topic:

Scripture:

Request:

Answer:

_____

ADORE GOD IN PRAYER

"Don't worry about anything;
instead, pray about everything" — Philippians 4:6 NIV

SIX SECRETS TO A POWERFUL QUIET TIME ©2005

*Prayer for*_____

Date: Topic:

Scripture:

Request:

Answer:

_____

Date: Topic:

Scripture:

Request:

Answer:

_____

Date: Topic:

Scripture:

Request:

Answer:

_____

Date: Topic:

Scripture:

Request:

Answer:

_____

Date: Topic:

Scripture:

Request:

Answer:

_____

ADORE GOD IN PRAYER

"Don't worry about anything; instead, pray about everything" — Philippians 4:6 NIV

*Prayer for*_____

Date: Topic:

Scripture:

Request:

Answer:

Date: Topic:

Scripture:

Request:

Answer:

Date: Topic:

Scripture:

Request:

Answer:

Date: Topic:

Scripture:

Request:

Answer:

Date: Topic:

Scripture:

Request:

Answer:

ADORE GOD IN PRAYER

"Don't worry about anything;
instead, pray about everything" — Philippians 4:6 NIV

SIX SECRETS TO A POWERFUL QUIET TIME ©2005

*Prayer for*_____

Date: Topic:
Scripture:
Request:

Answer:

Date: Topic:
Scripture:
Request:

Answer:

Date: Topic:
Scripture:
Request:

Answer:

Date: Topic:
Scripture:
Request:

Answer:

Date: Topic:
Scripture:
Request:

Answer:

ADORE GOD IN PRAYER

"Don't worry about anything; instead, pray about everything" — Philippians 4:6 NIV

SIX SECRETS TO A POWERFUL QUIET TIME ©2005

Prayer for_____

Date: Topic:

Scripture:

Request:

Answer:

_____

Date: Topic:

Scripture:

Request:

Answer:

_____

Date: Topic:

Scripture:

Request:

Answer:

_____

Date: Topic:

Scripture:

Request:

Answer:

_____

Date: Topic:

Scripture:

Request:

Answer:

_____

ADORE GOD IN PRAYER

"Don't worry about anything;
instead, pray about everything" — Philippians 4:6 NIV

SIX SECRETS TO A POWERFUL QUIET TIME ©2005

*Prayer for*_____

Date: Topic:

Scripture:

Request:

Answer:

_____

Date: Topic:

Scripture:

Request:

Answer:

_____

Date: Topic:

Scripture:

Request:

Answer:

_____

Date: Topic:

Scripture:

Request:

Answer:

_____

Date: Topic:

Scripture:

Request:

Answer:

_____

ADORE GOD IN PRAYER

"Don't worry about anything;
instead, pray about everything" — Philippians 4:6 NIV

SIX SECRETS TO A POWERFUL QUIET TIME. ©2005

*Prayer for*_____

Date: Topic:
Scripture:
Request:

Answer:

Date: Topic:
Scripture:
Request:

Answer:

Date: Topic:
Scripture:
Request:

Answer:

Date: Topic:
Scripture:
Request:

Answer:

Date: Topic:
Scripture:
Request:

Answer:

ADORE GOD IN PRAYER

"Don't worry about anything;
instead, pray about everything" — Philippians 4:6 NIV

*Prayer for*_____

Date: Topic:
Scripture:
Request:

Answer:

_____

Date: Topic:
Scripture:
Request:

Answer:

_____

Date: Topic:
Scripture:
Request:

Answer:

_____

Date: Topic:
Scripture:
Request:

Answer:

_____

Date: Topic:
Scripture:
Request:

Answer:

_____

ADORE GOD IN PRAYER

"Don't worry about anything;
instead, pray about everything" — Philippians 4:6 NIV

SIX SECRETS TO A POWERFUL QUIET TIME ©2005

Prayer for _____

Date: Topic:
Scripture:
Request:

Answer:

_____

Date: Topic:
Scripture:
Request:

Answer:

_____

Date: Topic:
Scripture:
Request:

Answer:

_____

Date: Topic:
Scripture:
Request:

Answer:

_____

Date: Topic:
Scripture:
Request:

Answer:

_____

*Prayer for*_____

Date: Topic:
Scripture:
Request:

Answer:

_____

Date: Topic:
Scripture:
Request:

Answer:

_____

Date: Topic:
Scripture:
Request:

Answer:

_____

Date: Topic:
Scripture:
Request:

Answer:

_____

Date: Topic:
Scripture:
Request:

Answer:

_____

ADORE GOD IN PRAYER

"Don't worry about anything; instead, pray about everything" — Philippians 4:6 NIV

*Prayer for*_____

Date: Topic:

Scripture:

Request:

Answer:

_____

Date: Topic:

Scripture:

Request:

Answer:

_____

Date: Topic:

Scripture:

Request:

Answer:

_____

Date: Topic:

Scripture:

Request:

Answer:

_____

Date: Topic:

Scripture:

Request:

Answer:

_____

ADORE GOD IN PRAYER

"Don't worry about anything;
instead, pray about everything" — Philippians 4:6 NIV

SIX SECRETS TO A POWERFUL QUIET TIME ©2005

*Prayer for*_____

Date: Topic:
Scripture:
Request:

Answer:

_____

Date: Topic:
Scripture:
Request:

Answer:

_____

Date: Topic:
Scripture:
Request:

Answer:

_____

Date: Topic:
Scripture:
Request:

Answer:

_____

Date: Topic:
Scripture:
Request:

Answer:

_____

YIELD — ENJOY — REST

"...let us run with perseverance the race marked out for us. Let us fix our eyes on Jesus, the author and perfecter of our faith..." — Hebrews 12:1-2 NIV

SIX SECRETS TO A POWERFUL QUIET TIME ©2005

Date _____

As you close your quiet time, spend a few moments in reflection — applying the truth of the Word of God in your own relationship with the Lord.

Yield Yourself to God

Place any unfulfilled dreams and desires in the hands of the Lord. If you sense a particular need today to humble yourself under God's mighty hand, that he may lift you up in due time (1 Peter 5:6), write a brief prayer expressing all that is on your heart.

Enjoy His Presence

Place today's activities, appointments, and responsibilities in the hands of the Lord.

Special Requests for Today —

One Significant Insight to Think About Today —

Rest in His Love

As you close your time with the Lord, place any anxious thoughts, conflicts, or difficult circumstances in the hands of the Lord. record a promise or verse from God's Word related to your particular need.

YIELD — ENJOY — REST

"...let us run with perseverance the race marked out for us. Let us fix our eyes on Jesus, the author and perfecter of our faith..." — Hebrews 12:1-2 NIV

SIX SECRETS TO A POWERFUL QUIET TIME ©2005

Date _____

As you close your quiet time, spend a few moments in reflection — applying the truth of the Word of God in your own relationship with the Lord.

Yield Yourself to God

Place any unfulfilled dreams and desires in the hands of the Lord. If you sense a particular need today to humble yourself under God's mighty hand, that he may lift you up in due time (1 Peter 5:6), write a brief prayer expressing all that is on your heart.

Enjoy His Presence

Place today's activities, appointments, and responsibilities in the hands of the Lord.

Special Requests for Today —

One Significant Insight to Think About Today —

Rest in His Love

As you close your time with the Lord, place any anxious thoughts, conflicts, or difficult circumstances in the hands of the Lord. record a promise or verse from God's Word related to your particular need.

YIELD — ENJOY — REST

"...let us run with perseverance the race marked out for us. Let us fix our eyes on Jesus, the author and perfecter of our faith..." — Hebrews 12:1-2 NIV

SIX SECRETS TO A POWERFUL QUIET TIME ©2005

Date _____

As you close your quiet time, spend a few moments in reflection — applying the truth of the Word of God in your own relationship with the Lord.

Yield Yourself to God

Place any unfulfilled dreams and desires in the hands of the Lord. If you sense a particular need today to humble yourself under God's mighty hand, that he may lift you up in due time (1 Peter 5:6), write a brief prayer expressing all that is on your heart.

Enjoy His Presence

Place today's activities, appointments, and responsibilities in the hands of the Lord.

Special Requests for Today —

One Significant Insight to Think About Today —

Rest in His Love

As you close your time with the Lord, place any anxious thoughts, conflicts, or difficult circumstances in the hands of the Lord. record a promise or verse from God's Word related to your particular need.

YIELD — ENJOY — REST

"...let us run with perseverance the race marked out for us. Let us fix our eyes on Jesus, the author and perfecter of our faith..." — Hebrews 12:1-2 NIV

SIX SECRETS TO A POWERFUL QUIET TIME ©2005

Date _____

As you close your quiet time, spend a few moments in reflection — applying the truth of the Word of God in your own relationship with the Lord.

Yield Yourself to God

Place any unfulfilled dreams and desires in the hands of the Lord. If you sense a particular need today to humble yourself under God's mighty hand, that he may lift you up in due time (1 Peter 5:6), write a brief prayer expressing all that is on your heart.

Enjoy His Presence

Place today's activities, appointments, and responsibilities in the hands of the Lord.

Special Requests for Today —

One Significant Insight to Think About Today —

Rest in His Love

As you close your time with the Lord, place any anxious thoughts, conflicts, or difficult circumstances in the hands of the Lord. record a promise or verse from God's Word related to your particular need.

YIELD — ENJOY — REST

"...let us run with perseverance the race marked out for us. Let us fix our eyes on Jesus, the author and perfecter of our faith..." — Hebrews 12:1-2 NIV

SIX SECRETS TO A POWERFUL QUIET TIME ©2005

Date _____

As you close your quiet time, spend a few moments in reflection — applying the truth of the Word of God in your own relationship with the Lord.

Yield Yourself to God

Place any unfulfilled dreams and desires in the hands of the Lord. If you sense a particular need today to humble yourself under God's mighty hand, that he may lift you up in due time (1 Peter 5:6), write a brief prayer expressing all that is on your heart.

Enjoy His Presence

Place today's activities, appointments, and responsibilities in the hands of the Lord.

Special Requests for Today —

One Significant Insight to Think About Today —

Rest in His Love

As you close your time with the Lord, place any anxious thoughts, conflicts, or difficult circumstances in the hands of the Lord. record a promise or verse from God's Word related to your particular need.

"...let us run with perseverance the race marked out for us. Let us fix our eyes on Jesus, the author and perfecter of our faith..." — Hebrews 12:1-2 NIV

SIX SECRETS TO A POWERFUL QUIET TIME ©2005

Date _____

As you close your quiet time, spend a few moments in reflection — applying the truth of the Word of God in your own relationship with the Lord.

Yield Yourself to God

Place any unfulfilled dreams and desires in the hands of the Lord. If you sense a particular need today to humble yourself under God's mighty hand, that he may lift you up in due time (1 Peter 5:6), write a brief prayer expressing all that is on your heart.

Enjoy His Presence

Place today's activities, appointments, and responsibilities in the hands of the Lord.

Special Requests for Today —

One Significant Insight to Think About Today —

Rest in His Love

As you close your time with the Lord, place any anxious thoughts, conflicts, or difficult circumstances in the hands of the Lord. record a promise or verse from God's Word related to your particular need.

YIELD — ENJOY — REST

"...let us run with perseverance the race marked out for us. Let us fix our eyes on Jesus, the author and perfecter of our faith..." — Hebrews 12:1-2 NIV

SIX SECRETS TO A POWERFUL QUIET TIME ©2005

Date _____

As you close your quiet time, spend a few moments in reflection — applying the truth of the Word of God in your own relationship with the Lord.

Yield Yourself to God

Place any unfulfilled dreams and desires in the hands of the Lord. If you sense a particular need today to humble yourself under God's mighty hand, that he may lift you up in due time (1 Peter 5:6), write a brief prayer expressing all that is on your heart.

Enjoy His Presence

Place today's activities, appointments, and responsibilities in the hands of the Lord.

Special Requests for Today —

One Significant Insight to Think About Today —

Rest in His Love

As you close your time with the Lord, place any anxious thoughts, conflicts, or difficult circumstances in the hands of the Lord. record a promise or verse from God's Word related to your particular need.

YIELD — ENJOY — REST

"...let us run with perseverance the race marked out for us. Let us fix our eyes on Jesus, the author and perfecter of our faith..." — Hebrews 12:1-2 NIV

SIX SECRETS TO A POWERFUL QUIET TIME ©2005

Date _____

As you close your quiet time, spend a few moments in reflection — applying the truth of the Word of God in your own relationship with the Lord.

Yield Yourself to God

Place any unfulfilled dreams and desires in the hands of the Lord. If you sense a particular need today to humble yourself under God's mighty hand, that he may lift you up in due time (1 Peter 5:6), write a brief prayer expressing all that is on your heart.

Enjoy His Presence

Place today's activities, appointments, and responsibilities in the hands of the Lord.

Special Requests for Today —

One Significant Insight to Think About Today —

Rest in His Love

As you close your time with the Lord, place any anxious thoughts, conflicts, or difficult circumstances in the hands of the Lord. record a promise or verse from God's Word related to your particular need.

YIELD — ENJOY — REST

"...let us run with perseverance the race marked out for us. Let us fix our eyes on Jesus, the author and perfecter of our faith..." — Hebrews 12:1-2 NIV

Date _____

As you close your quiet time, spend a few moments in reflection — applying the truth of the Word of God in your own relationship with the Lord.

Yield Yourself to God

Place any unfulfilled dreams and desires in the hands of the Lord. If you sense a particular need today to humble yourself under God's mighty hand, that he may lift you up in due time (1 Peter 5:6), write a brief prayer expressing all that is on your heart.

Enjoy His Presence

Place today's activities, appointments, and responsibilities in the hands of the Lord.

Special Requests for Today —

One Significant Insight to Think About Today —

Rest in His Love

As you close your time with the Lord, place any anxious thoughts, conflicts, or difficult circumstances in the hands of the Lord. record a promise or verse from God's Word related to your particular need.

YIELD — ENJOY — REST

"...let us run with perseverance the race marked out for us. Let us fix our eyes on Jesus, the author and perfecter of our faith..." — Hebrews 12:1-2 NIV

SIX SECRETS TO A POWERFUL QUIET TIME ©2005

Date _____

As you close your quiet time, spend a few moments in reflection — applying the truth of the Word of God in your own relationship with the Lord.

Yield Yourself to God

Place any unfulfilled dreams and desires in the hands of the Lord. If you sense a particular need today to humble yourself under God's mighty hand, that he may lift you up in due time (1 Peter 5:6), write a brief prayer expressing all that is on your heart.

Enjoy His Presence

Place today's activities, appointments, and responsibilities in the hands of the Lord.

Special Requests for Today —

One Significant Insight to Think About Today —

Rest in His Love

As you close your time with the Lord, place any anxious thoughts, conflicts, or difficult circumstances in the hands of the Lord. record a promise or verse from God's Word related to your particular need.

YIELD — ENJOY — REST

"...let us run with perseverance the race marked out for us. Let us fix our eyes on Jesus, the author and perfecter of our faith..." — Hebrews 12:1-2 NIV

SIX SECRETS TO A POWERFUL QUIET TIME ©2005

Date _____

As you close your quiet time, spend a few moments in reflection — applying the truth of the Word of God in your own relationship with the Lord.

Yield Yourself to God

Place any unfulfilled dreams and desires in the hands of the Lord. If you sense a particular need today to humble yourself under God's mighty hand, that he may lift you up in due time (1 Peter 5:6), write a brief prayer expressing all that is on your heart.

Enjoy His Presence

Place today's activities, appointments, and responsibilities in the hands of the Lord.

Special Requests for Today —

One Significant Insight to Think About Today —

Rest in His Love

As you close your time with the Lord, place any anxious thoughts, conflicts, or difficult circumstances in the hands of the Lord. record a promise or verse from God's Word related to your particular need.

YIELD — ENJOY — REST

"...let us run with perseverance the race marked out for us. Let us fix our eyes on Jesus, the author and perfecter of our faith..." — Hebrews 12:1-2 NIV

SIX SECRETS TO A POWERFUL QUIET TIME ©2005

Date _____

As you close your quiet time, spend a few moments in reflection — applying the truth of the Word of God in your own relationship with the Lord.

Yield Yourself to God

Place any unfulfilled dreams and desires in the hands of the Lord. If you sense a particular need today to humble yourself under God's mighty hand, that he may lift you up in due time (1 Peter 5:6), write a brief prayer expressing all that is on your heart.

Enjoy His Presence

Place today's activities, appointments, and responsibilities in the hands of the Lord.

Special Requests for Today —

One Significant Insight to Think About Today —

Rest in His Love

As you close your time with the Lord, place any anxious thoughts, conflicts, or difficult circumstances in the hands of the Lord. record a promise or verse from God's Word related to your particular need.

YIELD — ENJOY — REST

"...let us run with perseverance the race marked out for us. Let us fix our eyes on Jesus, the author and perfecter of our faith..." — Hebrews 12:1-2 NIV
— SIX SECRETS TO A POWERFUL QUIET TIME ©2005

Date _____

As you close your quiet time, spend a few moments in reflection — applying the truth of the Word of God in your own relationship with the Lord.

Yield Yourself to God

Place any unfulfilled dreams and desires in the hands of the Lord. If you sense a particular need today to humble yourself under God's mighty hand, that he may lift you up in due time (1 Peter 5:6), write a brief prayer expressing all that is on your heart.

Enjoy His Presence

Place today's activities, appointments, and responsibilities in the hands of the Lord.

Special Requests for Today —

One Significant Insight to Think About Today —

Rest in His Love

As you close your time with the Lord, place any anxious thoughts, conflicts, or difficult circumstances in the hands of the Lord. record a promise or verse from God's Word related to your particular need.

YIELD — ENJOY — REST

"...let us run with perseverance the race marked out for us. Let us fix our eyes on Jesus, the author and perfecter of our faith..." — Hebrews 12:1-2 NIV

SIX SECRETS TO A POWERFUL QUIET TIME ©2005

Date _____

As you close your quiet time, spend a few moments in reflection — applying the truth of the Word of God in your own relationship with the Lord.

Yield Yourself to God

Place any unfulfilled dreams and desires in the hands of the Lord. If you sense a particular need today to humble yourself under God's mighty hand, that he may lift you up in due time (1 Peter 5:6), write a brief prayer expressing all that is on your heart.

Enjoy His Presence

Place today's activities, appointments, and responsibilities in the hands of the Lord.

Special Requests for Today —

One Significant Insight to Think About Today —

Rest in His Love

As you close your time with the Lord, place any anxious thoughts, conflicts, or difficult circumstances in the hands of the Lord. record a promise or verse from God's Word related to your particular need.

YIELD — ENJOY — REST

"...let us run with perseverance the race marked out for us. Let us fix our eyes on Jesus, the author and perfecter of our faith..." — Hebrews 12:1-2 NIV

SIX SECRETS TO A POWERFUL QUIET TIME ©2005

Date _____

As you close your quiet time, spend a few moments in reflection — applying the truth of the Word of God in your own relationship with the Lord.

Yield Yourself to God

Place any unfulfilled dreams and desires in the hands of the Lord. If you sense a particular need today to humble yourself under God's mighty hand, that he may lift you up in due time (1 Peter 5:6), write a brief prayer expressing all that is on your heart.

Enjoy His Presence

Place today's activities, appointments, and responsibilities in the hands of the Lord.

Special Requests for Today —

One Significant Insight to Think About Today —

Rest in His Love

As you close your time with the Lord, place any anxious thoughts, conflicts, or difficult circumstances in the hands of the Lord. record a promise or verse from God's Word related to your particular need.

Date _____

*As you close your quiet time, spend a few moments in reflection — applying the truth of the Word of
God in your own relationship with the Lord.*

Yield Yourself to God

*Place any unfulfilled dreams and desires in the hands of the Lord. If you sense a particular need today
to humble yourself under God's mighty hand, that he may lift you up in due time (1 Peter 5:6), write
a brief prayer expressing all that is on your heart.*

Enjoy His Presence

Place today's activities, appointments, and responsibilities in the hands of the Lord.

Special Requests for Today —

One Significant Insight to Think About Today —

Rest in His Love

*As you close your time with the Lord, place any anxious thoughts, conflicts, or difficult circumstances
in the hands of the Lord. record a promise or verse from God's Word related to your particular need.*

YIELD — ENJOY — REST

"...let us run with perseverance the race marked out for us. Let us fix our eyes on Jesus, the author and perfecter of our faith..." — Hebrews 12:1-2 NIV

SIX SECRETS TO A POWERFUL QUIET TIME ©2005

Date _____

As you close your quiet time, spend a few moments in reflection — applying the truth of the Word of God in your own relationship with the Lord.

Yield Yourself to God

Place any unfulfilled dreams and desires in the hands of the Lord. If you sense a particular need today to humble yourself under God's mighty hand, that he may lift you up in due time (1 Peter 5:6), write a brief prayer expressing all that is on your heart.

Enjoy His Presence

Place today's activities, appointments, and responsibilities in the hands of the Lord.

Special Requests for Today —

One Significant Insight to Think About Today —

Rest in His Love

As you close your time with the Lord, place any anxious thoughts, conflicts, or difficult circumstances in the hands of the Lord. record a promise or verse from God's Word related to your particular need.

YIELD — ENJOY — REST

"...let us run with perseverance the race marked out for
us. Let us fix our eyes on Jesus, the author and perfecter
of our faith..." — Hebrews 12:1-2 NIV

SIX SECRETS TO A POWERFUL QUIET TIME ©2005

Date _____

As you close your quiet time, spend a few moments in reflection — applying the truth of the Word of God in your own relationship with the Lord.

Yield Yourself to God

Place any unfulfilled dreams and desires in the hands of the Lord. If you sense a particular need today to humble yourself under God's mighty hand, that he may lift you up in due time (1 Peter 5:6), write a brief prayer expressing all that is on your heart.

Enjoy His Presence

Place today's activities, appointments, and responsibilities in the hands of the Lord.

Special Requests for Today —

One Significant Insight to Think About Today —

Rest in His Love

As you close your time with the Lord, place any anxious thoughts, conflicts, or difficult circumstances in the hands of the Lord. record a promise or verse from God's Word related to your particular need.

YIELD — ENJOY — REST

"...let us run with perseverance the race marked out for us. Let us fix our eyes on Jesus, the author and perfecter of our faith..." — Hebrews 12:1-2 NIV

SIX SECRETS TO A POWERFUL QUIET TIME ©2005

Date _____

As you close your quiet time, spend a few moments in reflection — applying the truth of the Word of God in your own relationship with the Lord.

Yield Yourself to God

Place any unfulfilled dreams and desires in the hands of the Lord. If you sense a particular need today to humble yourself under God's mighty hand, that he may lift you up in due time (1 Peter 5:6), write a brief prayer expressing all that is on your heart.

Enjoy His Presence

Place today's activities, appointments, and responsibilities in the hands of the Lord.

Special Requests for Today —

One Significant Insight to Think About Today —

Rest in His Love

As you close your time with the Lord, place any anxious thoughts, conflicts, or difficult circumstances in the hands of the Lord. record a promise or verse from God's Word related to your particular need.

YIELD — ENJOY — REST

"...let us run with perseverance the race marked out for us. Let us fix our eyes on Jesus, the author and perfecter of our faith..." — Hebrews 12:1-2 NIV

SIX SECRETS TO A POWERFUL QUIET TIME ©2005

Date _____

As you close your quiet time, spend a few moments in reflection — applying the truth of the Word of God in your own relationship with the Lord.

Yield Yourself to God

Place any unfulfilled dreams and desires in the hands of the Lord. If you sense a particular need today to humble yourself under God's mighty hand, that he may lift you up in due time (1 Peter 5:6), write a brief prayer expressing all that is on your heart.

Enjoy His Presence

Place today's activities, appointments, and responsibilities in the hands of the Lord.

Special Requests for Today —

One Significant Insight to Think About Today —

Rest in His Love

As you close your time with the Lord, place any anxious thoughts, conflicts, or difficult circumstances in the hands of the Lord. record a promise or verse from God's Word related to your particular need.

YIELD — ENJOY — REST

"...let us run with perseverance the race marked out for us. Let us fix our eyes on Jesus, the author and perfecter of our faith..." — Hebrews 12:1-2 NIV

SIX SECRETS TO A POWERFUL QUIET TIME ©2005

Date _____

As you close your quiet time, spend a few moments in reflection — applying the truth of the Word of God in your own relationship with the Lord.

Yield Yourself to God

Place any unfulfilled dreams and desires in the hands of the Lord. If you sense a particular need today to humble yourself under God's mighty hand, that he may lift you up in due time (1 Peter 5:6), write a brief prayer expressing all that is on your heart.

Enjoy His Presence

Place today's activities, appointments, and responsibilities in the hands of the Lord.

Special Requests for Today —

One Significant Insight to Think About Today —

Rest in His Love

As you close your time with the Lord, place any anxious thoughts, conflicts, or difficult circumstances in the hands of the Lord. record a promise or verse from God's Word related to your particular need.

YIELD — ENJOY — REST

"...let us run with perseverance the race marked out for us. Let us fix our eyes on Jesus, the author and perfecter of our faith..." — Hebrews 12:1-2 NIV

SIX SECRETS TO A POWERFUL QUIET TIME ©2005

Date _____

As you close your quiet time, spend a few moments in reflection — applying the truth of the Word of God in your own relationship with the Lord.

Yield Yourself to God

Place any unfulfilled dreams and desires in the hands of the Lord. If you sense a particular need today to humble yourself under God's mighty hand, that he may lift you up in due time (1 Peter 5:6), write a brief prayer expressing all that is on your heart.

Enjoy His Presence

Place today's activities, appointments, and responsibilities in the hands of the Lord.

Special Requests for Today —

One Significant Insight to Think About Today —

Rest in His Love

As you close your time with the Lord, place any anxious thoughts, conflicts, or difficult circumstances in the hands of the Lord. record a promise or verse from God's Word related to your particular need.

YIELD — ENJOY — REST

"...let us run with perseverance the race marked out for us. Let us fix our eyes on Jesus, the author and perfecter of our faith..." — Hebrews 12:1-2 NIV

SIX SECRETS TO A POWERFUL QUIET TIME ©2005

Date _____

As you close your quiet time, spend a few moments in reflection — applying the truth of the Word of God in your own relationship with the Lord.

Yield Yourself to God

Place any unfulfilled dreams and desires in the hands of the Lord. If you sense a particular need today to humble yourself under God's mighty hand, that he may lift you up in due time (1 Peter 5:6), write a brief prayer expressing all that is on your heart.

Enjoy His Presence

Place today's activities, appointments, and responsibilities in the hands of the Lord.

Special Requests for Today —

One Significant Insight to Think About Today —

Rest in His Love

As you close your time with the Lord, place any anxious thoughts, conflicts, or difficult circumstances in the hands of the Lord. record a promise or verse from God's Word related to your particular need.

YIELD — ENJOY — REST

"...let us run with perseverance the race marked out for us. Let us fix our eyes on Jesus, the author and perfecter of our faith..." — Hebrews 12:1-2 NIV

SIX SECRETS TO A POWERFUL QUIET TIME ©2005

Date _____

As you close your quiet time, spend a few moments in reflection — applying the truth of the Word of God in your own relationship with the Lord.

Yield Yourself to God

Place any unfulfilled dreams and desires in the hands of the Lord. If you sense a particular need today to humble yourself under God's mighty hand, that he may lift you up in due time (1 Peter 5:6), write a brief prayer expressing all that is on your heart.

Enjoy His Presence

Place today's activities, appointments, and responsibilities in the hands of the Lord.

Special Requests for Today —

One Significant Insight to Think About Today —

Rest in His Love

As you close your time with the Lord, place any anxious thoughts, conflicts, or difficult circumstances in the hands of the Lord. record a promise or verse from God's Word related to your particular need.

YIELD — ENJOY — REST

"...let us run with perseverance the race marked out for us. Let us fix our eyes on Jesus, the author and perfecter of our faith..." — Hebrews 12:1-2 NIV

SIX SECRETS TO A POWERFUL QUIET TIME ©2005

Date _____

As you close your quiet time, spend a few moments in reflection — applying the truth of the Word of God in your own relationship with the Lord.

Yield Yourself to God

Place any unfulfilled dreams and desires in the hands of the Lord. If you sense a particular need today to humble yourself under God's mighty hand, that he may lift you up in due time (1 Peter 5:6), write a brief prayer expressing all that is on your heart.

Enjoy His Presence

Place today's activities, appointments, and responsibilities in the hands of the Lord.

Special Requests for Today —

One Significant Insight to Think About Today —

Rest in His Love

As you close your time with the Lord, place any anxious thoughts, conflicts, or difficult circumstances in the hands of the Lord. record a promise or verse from God's Word related to your particular need.

YIELD — ENJOY — REST

"...let us run with perseverance the race marked out for us. Let us fix our eyes on Jesus, the author and perfecter of our faith..." — Hebrews 12:1-2 NIV

SIX SECRETS TO A POWERFUL QUIET TIME ©2005

Date _____

As you close your quiet time, spend a few moments in reflection — applying the truth of the Word of God in your own relationship with the Lord.

Yield Yourself to God

Place any unfulfilled dreams and desires in the hands of the Lord. If you sense a particular need today to humble yourself under God's mighty hand, that he may lift you up in due time (1 Peter 5:6), write a brief prayer expressing all that is on your heart.

Enjoy His Presence

Place today's activities, appointments, and responsibilities in the hands of the Lord.

Special Requests for Today —

One Significant Insight to Think About Today —

Rest in His Love

As you close your time with the Lord, place any anxious thoughts, conflicts, or difficult circumstances in the hands of the Lord. record a promise or verse from God's Word related to your particular need.

YIELD — ENJOY — REST

"...let us run with perseverance the race marked out for us. Let us fix our eyes on Jesus, the author and perfecter of our faith..." — Hebrews 12:1-2 NIV

SIX SECRETS TO A POWERFUL QUIET TIME ©2005

Date _____

As you close your quiet time, spend a few moments in reflection — applying the truth of the Word of God in your own relationship with the Lord.

Yield Yourself to God

Place any unfulfilled dreams and desires in the hands of the Lord. If you sense a particular need today to humble yourself under God's mighty hand, that he may lift you up in due time (1 Peter 5:6), write a brief prayer expressing all that is on your heart.

Enjoy His Presence

Place today's activities, appointments, and responsibilities in the hands of the Lord.

Special Requests for Today —

One Significant Insight to Think About Today —

Rest in His Love

As you close your time with the Lord, place any anxious thoughts, conflicts, or difficult circumstances in the hands of the Lord. record a promise or verse from God's Word related to your particular need.

YIELD — ENJOY — REST

"...let us run with perseverance the race marked out for us. Let us fix our eyes on Jesus, the author and perfecter of our faith..." — Hebrews 12:1-2 NIV

SIX SECRETS TO A POWERFUL QUIET TIME ©2005

Date _____

As you close your quiet time, spend a few moments in reflection — applying the truth of the Word of God in your own relationship with the Lord.

Yield Yourself to God

Place any unfulfilled dreams and desires in the hands of the Lord. If you sense a particular need today to humble yourself under God's mighty hand, that he may lift you up in due time (1 Peter 5:6), write a brief prayer expressing all that is on your heart.

Enjoy His Presence

Place today's activities, appointments, and responsibilities in the hands of the Lord.

Special Requests for Today —

One Significant Insight to Think About Today —

Rest in His Love

As you close your time with the Lord, place any anxious thoughts, conflicts, or difficult circumstances in the hands of the Lord. record a promise or verse from God's Word related to your particular need.

YIELD — ENJOY — REST

"...let us run with perseverance the race marked out for us. Let us fix our eyes on Jesus, the author and perfecter of our faith..." — Hebrews 12:1-2 NIV

SIX SECRETS TO A POWERFUL QUIET TIME ©2005

Date _____

As you close your quiet time, spend a few moments in reflection — applying the truth of the Word of God in your own relationship with the Lord.

Yield Yourself to God

Place any unfulfilled dreams and desires in the hands of the Lord. If you sense a particular need today to humble yourself under God's mighty hand, that he may lift you up in due time (1 Peter 5:6), write a brief prayer expressing all that is on your heart.

Enjoy His Presence

Place today's activities, appointments, and responsibilities in the hands of the Lord.

Special Requests for Today —

One Significant Insight to Think About Today —

Rest in His Love

As you close your time with the Lord, place any anxious thoughts, conflicts, or difficult circumstances in the hands of the Lord. record a promise or verse from God's Word related to your particular need.

YIELD — ENJOY — REST

"...let us run with perseverance the race marked out for us. Let us fix our eyes on Jesus, the author and perfecter of our faith..." — Hebrews 12:1-2 NIV

SIX SECRETS TO A POWERFUL QUIET TIME ©2005

Date _____

As you close your quiet time, spend a few moments in reflection — applying the truth of the Word of God in your own relationship with the Lord.

Yield Yourself to God

Place any unfulfilled dreams and desires in the hands of the Lord. If you sense a particular need today to humble yourself under God's mighty hand, that he may lift you up in due time (1 Peter 5:6), write a brief prayer expressing all that is on your heart.

Enjoy His Presence

Place today's activities, appointments, and responsibilities in the hands of the Lord.

Special Requests for Today —

One Significant Insight to Think About Today —

Rest in His Love

As you close your time with the Lord, place any anxious thoughts, conflicts, or difficult circumstances in the hands of the Lord. record a promise or verse from God's Word related to your particular need.

YIELD — ENJOY — REST

"...let us run with perseverance the race marked out for us. Let us fix our eyes on Jesus, the author and perfecter of our faith..." — Hebrews 12:1-2 NIV

SIX SECRETS TO A POWERFUL QUIET TIME ©2005

Date _____

As you close your quiet time, spend a few moments in reflection — applying the truth of the Word of God in your own relationship with the Lord.

Yield Yourself to God

Place any unfulfilled dreams and desires in the hands of the Lord. If you sense a particular need today to humble yourself under God's mighty hand, that he may lift you up in due time (1 Peter 5:6), write a brief prayer expressing all that is on your heart.

Enjoy His Presence

Place today's activities, appointments, and responsibilities in the hands of the Lord.

Special Requests for Today —

One Significant Insight to Think About Today —

Rest in His Love

As you close your time with the Lord, place any anxious thoughts, conflicts, or difficult circumstances in the hands of the Lord. record a promise or verse from God's Word related to your particular need.

YIELD — ENJOY — REST

"...let us run with perseverance the race marked out for us. Let us fix our eyes on Jesus, the author and perfecter of our faith..." — Hebrews 12:1-2 NIV

Date _____

As you close your quiet time, spend a few moments in reflection — applying the truth of the Word of God in your own relationship with the Lord.

Yield Yourself to God

Place any unfulfilled dreams and desires in the hands of the Lord. If you sense a particular need today to humble yourself under God's mighty hand, that he may lift you up in due time (1 Peter 5:6), write a brief prayer expressing all that is on your heart.

Enjoy His Presence

Place today's activities, appointments, and responsibilities in the hands of the Lord.

Special Requests for Today —

One Significant Insight to Think About Today —

Rest in His Love

As you close your time with the Lord, place any anxious thoughts, conflicts, or difficult circumstances in the hands of the Lord. record a promise or verse from God's Word related to your particular need.

YIELD — ENJOY — REST

"...let us run with perseverance the race marked out for us. Let us fix our eyes on Jesus, the author and perfecter of our faith..." — Hebrews 12:1-2 NIV

SIX SECRETS TO A POWERFUL QUIET TIME ©2005

Date _____

As you close your quiet time, spend a few moments in reflection — applying the truth of the Word of God in your own relationship with the Lord.

Yield Yourself to God

Place any unfulfilled dreams and desires in the hands of the Lord. If you sense a particular need today to humble yourself under God's mighty hand, that he may lift you up in due time (1 Peter 5:6), write a brief prayer expressing all that is on your heart.

Enjoy His Presence

Place today's activities, appointments, and responsibilities in the hands of the Lord.

Special Requests for Today —

One Significant Insight to Think About Today —

Rest in His Love

As you close your time with the Lord, place any anxious thoughts, conflicts, or difficult circumstances in the hands of the Lord. record a promise or verse from God's Word related to your particular need.

YIELD — ENJOY — REST

"...let us run with perseverance the race marked out for us. Let us fix our eyes on Jesus, the author and perfecter of our faith..." — Hebrews 12:1-2 NIV

SIX SECRETS TO A POWERFUL QUIET TIME ©2005

Date _____

As you close your quiet time, spend a few moments in reflection — applying the truth of the Word of God in your own relationship with the Lord.

Yield Yourself to God

Place any unfulfilled dreams and desires in the hands of the Lord. If you sense a particular need today to humble yourself under God's mighty hand, that he may lift you up in due time (1 Peter 5:6), write a brief prayer expressing all that is on your heart.

Enjoy His Presence

Place today's activities, appointments, and responsibilities in the hands of the Lord.

Special Requests for Today —

One Significant Insight to Think About Today —

Rest in His Love

As you close your time with the Lord, place any anxious thoughts, conflicts, or difficult circumstances in the hands of the Lord. record a promise or verse from God's Word related to your particular need.

YIELD — ENJOY — REST

"...let us run with perseverance the race marked out for us. Let us fix our eyes on Jesus, the author and perfecter of our faith..." — Hebrews 12:1-2 NIV

SIX SECRETS TO A POWERFUL QUIET TIME ©2005

Date _____

As you close your quiet time, spend a few moments in reflection — applying the truth of the Word of God in your own relationship with the Lord.

Yield Yourself to God

Place any unfulfilled dreams and desires in the hands of the Lord. If you sense a particular need today to humble yourself under God's mighty hand, that he may lift you up in due time (1 Peter 5:6), write a brief prayer expressing all that is on your heart.

Enjoy His Presence

Place today's activities, appointments, and responsibilities in the hands of the Lord.

Special Requests for Today —

One Significant Insight to Think About Today —

Rest in His Love

As you close your time with the Lord, place any anxious thoughts, conflicts, or difficult circumstances in the hands of the Lord. record a promise or verse from God's Word related to your particular need.

YIELD — ENJOY — REST

"...let us run with perseverance the race marked out for us. Let us fix our eyes on Jesus, the author and perfecter of our faith..." — Hebrews 12:1-2 NIV

SIX SECRETS TO A POWERFUL QUIET TIME ©2005

Date _____

As you close your quiet time, spend a few moments in reflection — applying the truth of the Word of God in your own relationship with the Lord.

Yield Yourself to God

Place any unfulfilled dreams and desires in the hands of the Lord. If you sense a particular need today to humble yourself under God's mighty hand, that he may lift you up in due time (1 Peter 5:6), write a brief prayer expressing all that is on your heart.

Enjoy His Presence

Place today's activities, appointments, and responsibilities in the hands of the Lord.

Special Requests for Today —

One Significant Insight to Think About Today —

Rest in His Love

As you close your time with the Lord, place any anxious thoughts, conflicts, or difficult circumstances in the hands of the Lord. record a promise or verse from God's Word related to your particular need.

YIELD — ENJOY — REST

"...let us run with perseverance the race marked out for us. Let us fix our eyes on Jesus, the author and perfecter of our faith..." — Hebrews 12:1-2 NIV

SIX SECRETS TO A POWERFUL QUIET TIME ©2005

Date _____

As you close your quiet time, spend a few moments in reflection — applying the truth of the Word of God in your own relationship with the Lord.

Yield Yourself to God

Place any unfulfilled dreams and desires in the hands of the Lord. If you sense a particular need today to humble yourself under God's mighty hand, that he may lift you up in due time (1 Peter 5:6), write a brief prayer expressing all that is on your heart.

Enjoy His Presence

Place today's activities, appointments, and responsibilities in the hands of the Lord.

Special Requests for Today —

One Significant Insight to Think About Today —

Rest in His Love

As you close your time with the Lord, place any anxious thoughts, conflicts, or difficult circumstances in the hands of the Lord. record a promise or verse from God's Word related to your particular need.

YIELD — ENJOY — REST

"...let us run with perseverance the race marked out for us. Let us fix our eyes on Jesus, the author and perfecter of our faith..." — Hebrews 12:1-2 NIV

SIX SECRETS TO A POWERFUL QUIET TIME ©2005

Date _____

As you close your quiet time, spend a few moments in reflection — applying the truth of the Word of God in your own relationship with the Lord.

Yield Yourself to God

Place any unfulfilled dreams and desires in the hands of the Lord. If you sense a particular need today to humble yourself under God's mighty hand, that he may lift you up in due time (1 Peter 5:6), write a brief prayer expressing all that is on your heart.

Enjoy His Presence

Place today's activities, appointments, and responsibilities in the hands of the Lord.

Special Requests for Today —

One Significant Insight to Think About Today —

Rest in His Love

As you close your time with the Lord, place any anxious thoughts, conflicts, or difficult circumstances in the hands of the Lord. record a promise or verse from God's Word related to your particular need.

Date _____

As you close your quiet time, spend a few moments in reflection — applying the truth of the Word of God in your own relationship with the Lord.

Yield Yourself to God

Place any unfulfilled dreams and desires in the hands of the Lord. If you sense a particular need today to humble yourself under God's mighty hand, that he may lift you up in due time (1 Peter 5:6), write a brief prayer expressing all that is on your heart.

Enjoy His Presence

Place today's activities, appointments, and responsibilities in the hands of the Lord.

Special Requests for Today —

One Significant Insight to Think About Today —

Rest in His Love

As you close your time with the Lord, place any anxious thoughts, conflicts, or difficult circumstances in the hands of the Lord. record a promise or verse from God's Word related to your particular need.

YIELD — ENJOY — REST

"...let us run with perseverance the race marked out for us. Let us fix our eyes on Jesus, the author and perfecter of our faith..." — Hebrews 12:1-2 NIV

SIX SECRETS TO A POWERFUL QUIET TIME ©2005

Date _____

As you close your quiet time, spend a few moments in reflection — applying the truth of the Word of God in your own relationship with the Lord.

Yield Yourself to God

Place any unfulfilled dreams and desires in the hands of the Lord. If you sense a particular need today to humble yourself under God's mighty hand, that he may lift you up in due time (1 Peter 5:6), write a brief prayer expressing all that is on your heart.

Enjoy His Presence

Place today's activities, appointments, and responsibilities in the hands of the Lord.

Special Requests for Today —

One Significant Insight to Think About Today —

Rest in His Love

As you close your time with the Lord, place any anxious thoughts, conflicts, or difficult circumstances in the hands of the Lord. record a promise or verse from God's Word related to your particular need.

YIELD — ENJOY — REST

"...let us run with perseverance the race marked out for us. Let us fix our eyes on Jesus, the author and perfecter of our faith..." — Hebrews 12:1-2 NIV

SIX SECRETS TO A POWERFUL QUIET TIME ©2005

Date _____

As you close your quiet time, spend a few moments in reflection — applying the truth of the Word of God in your own relationship with the Lord.

Yield Yourself to God

Place any unfulfilled dreams and desires in the hands of the Lord. If you sense a particular need today to humble yourself under God's mighty hand, that he may lift you up in due time (1 Peter 5:6), write a brief prayer expressing all that is on your heart.

Enjoy His Presence

Place today's activities, appointments, and responsibilities in the hands of the Lord.

Special Requests for Today —

One Significant Insight to Think About Today —

Rest in His Love

As you close your time with the Lord, place any anxious thoughts, conflicts, or difficult circumstances in the hands of the Lord. record a promise or verse from God's Word related to your particular need.

YIELD — ENJOY — REST

"...let us run with perseverance the race marked out for us. Let us fix our eyes on Jesus, the author and perfecter of our faith..." — Hebrews 12:1-2 NIV

SIX SECRETS TO A POWERFUL QUIET TIME ©2005

Date _____

As you close your quiet time, spend a few moments in reflection — applying the truth of the Word of God in your own relationship with the Lord.

Yield Yourself to God

Place any unfulfilled dreams and desires in the hands of the Lord. If you sense a particular need today to humble yourself under God's mighty hand, that he may lift you up in due time (1 Peter 5:6), write a brief prayer expressing all that is on your heart.

Enjoy His Presence

Place today's activities, appointments, and responsibilities in the hands of the Lord.

Special Requests for Today —

One Significant Insight to Think About Today —

Rest in His Love

As you close your time with the Lord, place any anxious thoughts, conflicts, or difficult circumstances in the hands of the Lord. record a promise or verse from God's Word related to your particular need.

YIELD — ENJOY — REST

"...let us run with perseverance the race marked out for us. Let us fix our eyes on Jesus, the author and perfecter of our faith..." — Hebrews 12:1-2 NIV

SIX SECRETS TO A POWERFUL QUIET TIME ©2005

Date _____

As you close your quiet time, spend a few moments in reflection — applying the truth of the Word of God in your own relationship with the Lord.

Yield Yourself to God

Place any unfulfilled dreams and desires in the hands of the Lord. If you sense a particular need today to humble yourself under God's mighty hand, that he may lift you up in due time (1 Peter 5:6), write a brief prayer expressing all that is on your heart.

Enjoy His Presence

Place today's activities, appointments, and responsibilities in the hands of the Lord.

Special Requests for Today —

One Significant Insight to Think About Today —

Rest in His Love

As you close your time with the Lord, place any anxious thoughts, conflicts, or difficult circumstances in the hands of the Lord. record a promise or verse from God's Word related to your particular need.

YIELD — ENJOY — REST

"...let us run with perseverance the race marked out for us. Let us fix our eyes on Jesus, the author and perfecter of our faith..." — Hebrews 12:1-2 NIV

SIX SECRETS TO A POWERFUL QUIET TIME ©2005

Date _____

As you close your quiet time, spend a few moments in reflection — applying the truth of the Word of God in your own relationship with the Lord.

Yield Yourself to God

Place any unfulfilled dreams and desires in the hands of the Lord. If you sense a particular need today to humble yourself under God's mighty hand, that he may lift you up in due time (1 Peter 5:6), write a brief prayer expressing all that is on your heart.

Enjoy His Presence

Place today's activities, appointments, and responsibilities in the hands of the Lord.

Special Requests for Today —

One Significant Insight to Think About Today —

Rest in His Love

As you close your time with the Lord, place any anxious thoughts, conflicts, or difficult circumstances in the hands of the Lord. record a promise or verse from God's Word related to your particular need.

YIELD — ENJOY — REST

"...let us run with perseverance the race marked out for us. Let us fix our eyes on Jesus, the author and perfecter of our faith..." — Hebrews 12:1-2 NIV

SIX SECRETS TO A POWERFUL QUIET TIME ©2005

Date _____

As you close your quiet time, spend a few moments in reflection — applying the truth of the Word of God in your own relationship with the Lord.

Yield Yourself to God

Place any unfulfilled dreams and desires in the hands of the Lord. If you sense a particular need today to humble yourself under God's mighty hand, that he may lift you up in due time (1 Peter 5:6), write a brief prayer expressing all that is on your heart.

Enjoy His Presence

Place today's activities, appointments, and responsibilities in the hands of the Lord.

Special Requests for Today —

One Significant Insight to Think About Today —

Rest in His Love

As you close your time with the Lord, place any anxious thoughts, conflicts, or difficult circumstances in the hands of the Lord. record a promise or verse from God's Word related to your particular need.

307

YIELD — ENJOY — REST

"...let us run with perseverance the race marked out for
us. Let us fix our eyes on Jesus, the author and perfecter
of our faith..." — Hebrews 12:1-2 NIV

SIX SECRETS TO A POWERFUL QUIET TIME ©2005

Date _____

*As you close your quiet time, spend a few moments in reflection — applying the truth of the Word of
God in your own relationship with the Lord.*

Yield Yourself to God

*Place any unfulfilled dreams and desires in the hands of the Lord. If you sense a particular need today
to humble yourself under God's mighty hand, that he may lift you up in due time (1 Peter 5:6), write
a brief prayer expressing all that is on your heart.*

Enjoy His Presence

Place today's activities, appointments, and responsibilities in the hands of the Lord.

Special Requests for Today —

One Significant Insight to Think About Today —

Rest in His Love

*As you close your time with the Lord, place any anxious thoughts, conflicts, or difficult circumstances
in the hands of the Lord. record a promise or verse from God's Word related to your particular need.*

Date _____

As you close your quiet time, spend a few moments in reflection — applying the truth of the Word of God in your own relationship with the Lord.

Yield Yourself to God

Place any unfulfilled dreams and desires in the hands of the Lord. If you sense a particular need today to humble yourself under God's mighty hand, that he may lift you up in due time (1 Peter 5:6), write a brief prayer expressing all that is on your heart.

Enjoy His Presence

Place today's activities, appointments, and responsibilities in the hands of the Lord.

Special Requests for Today —

One Significant Insight to Think About Today —

Rest in His Love

As you close your time with the Lord, place any anxious thoughts, conflicts, or difficult circumstances in the hands of the Lord. record a promise or verse from God's Word related to your particular need.

YIELD — ENJOY — REST

"...let us run with perseverance the race marked out for us. Let us fix our eyes on Jesus, the author and perfecter of our faith..." — Hebrews 12:1-2 NIV

SIX SECRETS TO A POWERFUL QUIET TIME ©2005

Date _____

As you close your quiet time, spend a few moments in reflection — applying the truth of the Word of God in your own relationship with the Lord.

Yield Yourself to God

Place any unfulfilled dreams and desires in the hands of the Lord. If you sense a particular need today to humble yourself under God's mighty hand, that he may lift you up in due time (1 Peter 5:6), write a brief prayer expressing all that is on your heart.

Enjoy His Presence

Place today's activities, appointments, and responsibilities in the hands of the Lord.

Special Requests for Today —

One Significant Insight to Think About Today —

Rest in His Love

As you close your time with the Lord, place any anxious thoughts, conflicts, or difficult circumstances in the hands of the Lord. record a promise or verse from God's Word related to your particular need.

"...let us run with perseverance the race marked out for us. Let us fix our eyes on Jesus, the author and perfecter of our faith..." — Hebrews 12:1-2 NIV

SIX SECRETS TO A POWERFUL QUIET TIME ©2005

Date _____

As you close your quiet time, spend a few moments in reflection — applying the truth of the Word of God in your own relationship with the Lord.

Yield Yourself to God

Place any unfulfilled dreams and desires in the hands of the Lord. If you sense a particular need today to humble yourself under God's mighty hand, that he may lift you up in due time (1 Peter 5:6), write a brief prayer expressing all that is on your heart.

Enjoy His Presence

Place today's activities, appointments, and responsibilities in the hands of the Lord.

Special Requests for Today —

One Significant Insight to Think About Today —

Rest in His Love

As you close your time with the Lord, place any anxious thoughts, conflicts, or difficult circumstances in the hands of the Lord. record a promise or verse from God's Word related to your particular need.

YIELD — ENJOY — REST

"...let us run with perseverance the race marked out for us. Let us fix our eyes on Jesus, the author and perfecter of our faith..." — Hebrews 12:1-2 NIV

SIX SECRETS TO A POWERFUL QUIET TIME ©2005

Date _____

As you close your quiet time, spend a few moments in reflection — applying the truth of the Word of God in your own relationship with the Lord.

Yield Yourself to God

Place any unfulfilled dreams and desires in the hands of the Lord. If you sense a particular need today to humble yourself under God's mighty hand, that he may lift you up in due time (1 Peter 5:6), write a brief prayer expressing all that is on your heart.

Enjoy His Presence

Place today's activities, appointments, and responsibilities in the hands of the Lord.

Special Requests for Today —

One Significant Insight to Think About Today —

Rest in His Love

As you close your time with the Lord, place any anxious thoughts, conflicts, or difficult circumstances in the hands of the Lord. record a promise or verse from God's Word related to your particular need.

YIELD — ENJOY — REST

"...let us run with perseverance the race marked out for us. Let us fix our eyes on Jesus, the author and perfecter of our faith..." — Hebrews 12:1-2 NIV

SIX SECRETS TO A POWERFUL QUIET TIME ©2005

Date _____

As you close your quiet time, spend a few moments in reflection — applying the truth of the Word of God in your own relationship with the Lord.

Yield Yourself to God

Place any unfulfilled dreams and desires in the hands of the Lord. If you sense a particular need today to humble yourself under God's mighty hand, that he may lift you up in due time (1 Peter 5:6), write a brief prayer expressing all that is on your heart.

Enjoy His Presence

Place today's activities, appointments, and responsibilities in the hands of the Lord.

Special Requests for Today —

One Significant Insight to Think About Today —

Rest in His Love

As you close your time with the Lord, place any anxious thoughts, conflicts, or difficult circumstances in the hands of the Lord. record a promise or verse from God's Word related to your particular need.

YIELD — ENJOY — REST

"...let us run with perseverance the race marked out for us. Let us fix our eyes on Jesus, the author and perfecter of our faith..." — Hebrews 12:1-2 NIV

SIX SECRETS TO A POWERFUL QUIET TIME ©2005

Date _____

As you close your quiet time, spend a few moments in reflection — applying the truth of the Word of God in your own relationship with the Lord.

Yield Yourself to God

Place any unfulfilled dreams and desires in the hands of the Lord. If you sense a particular need today to humble yourself under God's mighty hand, that he may lift you up in due time (1 Peter 5:6), write a brief prayer expressing all that is on your heart.

Enjoy His Presence

Place today's activities, appointments, and responsibilities in the hands of the Lord.

Special Requests for Today —

One Significant Insight to Think About Today —

Rest in His Love

As you close your time with the Lord, place any anxious thoughts, conflicts, or difficult circumstances in the hands of the Lord. record a promise or verse from God's Word related to your particular need.

"...let us run with perseverance the race marked out for us. Let us fix our eyes on Jesus, the author and perfecter of our faith..." — Hebrews 12:1-2 NIV

SIX SECRETS TO A POWERFUL QUIET TIME ©2005

Date _____

As you close your quiet time, spend a few moments in reflection — applying the truth of the Word of God in your own relationship with the Lord.

Yield Yourself to God

Place any unfulfilled dreams and desires in the hands of the Lord. If you sense a particular need today to humble yourself under God's mighty hand, that he may lift you up in due time (1 Peter 5:6), write a brief prayer expressing all that is on your heart.

Enjoy His Presence

Place today's activities, appointments, and responsibilities in the hands of the Lord.

Special Requests for Today —

One Significant Insight to Think About Today —

Rest in His Love

As you close your time with the Lord, place any anxious thoughts, conflicts, or difficult circumstances in the hands of the Lord. record a promise or verse from God's Word related to your particular need.

YIELD — ENJOY — REST

"...let us run with perseverance the race marked out for
us. Let us fix our eyes on Jesus, the author and perfecter
of our faith..." — Hebrews 12:1-2 NIV

SIX SECRETS TO A POWERFUL QUIET TIME ©2005

Date _____

*As you close your quiet time, spend a few moments in reflection — applying the truth of the Word of
God in your own relationship with the Lord.*

Yield Yourself to God

*Place any unfulfilled dreams and desires in the hands of the Lord. If you sense a particular need today
to humble yourself under God's mighty hand, that he may lift you up in due time (1 Peter 5:6), write
a brief prayer expressing all that is on your heart.*

Enjoy His Presence

Place today's activities, appointments, and responsibilities in the hands of the Lord.

Special Requests for Today —

One Significant Insight to Think About Today —

Rest in His Love

*As you close your time with the Lord, place any anxious thoughts, conflicts, or difficult circumstances
in the hands of the Lord. record a promise or verse from God's Word related to your particular need.*

"...let us run with perseverance the race marked out for us. Let us fix our eyes on Jesus, the author and perfecter of our faith..." — Hebrews 12:1-2 NIV

SIX SECRETS TO A POWERFUL QUIET TIME ©2005

Date _____

As you close your quiet time, spend a few moments in reflection — applying the truth of the Word of God in your own relationship with the Lord.

Yield Yourself to God

Place any unfulfilled dreams and desires in the hands of the Lord. If you sense a particular need today to humble yourself under God's mighty hand, that he may lift you up in due time (1 Peter 5:6), write a brief prayer expressing all that is on your heart.

Enjoy His Presence

Place today's activities, appointments, and responsibilities in the hands of the Lord.

Special Requests for Today —

One Significant Insight to Think About Today —

Rest in His Love

As you close your time with the Lord, place any anxious thoughts, conflicts, or difficult circumstances in the hands of the Lord. record a promise or verse from God's Word related to your particular need.

YIELD — ENJOY — REST

"...let us run with perseverance the race marked out for us. Let us fix our eyes on Jesus, the author and perfecter of our faith..." — Hebrews 12:1-2 NIV

SIX SECRETS TO A POWERFUL QUIET TIME ©2005

Date _____

As you close your quiet time, spend a few moments in reflection — applying the truth of the Word of God in your own relationship with the Lord.

Yield Yourself to God

Place any unfulfilled dreams and desires in the hands of the Lord. If you sense a particular need today to humble yourself under God's mighty hand, that he may lift you up in due time (1 Peter 5:6), write a brief prayer expressing all that is on your heart.

Enjoy His Presence

Place today's activities, appointments, and responsibilities in the hands of the Lord.

Special Requests for Today —

One Significant Insight to Think About Today —

Rest in His Love

As you close your time with the Lord, place any anxious thoughts, conflicts, or difficult circumstances in the hands of the Lord. record a promise or verse from God's Word related to your particular need.

YIELD — ENJOY — REST

"...let us run with perseverance the race marked out for us. Let us fix our eyes on Jesus, the author and perfecter of our faith..." — Hebrews 12:1-2 NIV

SIX SECRETS TO A POWERFUL QUIET TIME ©2005

Date _____

As you close your quiet time, spend a few moments in reflection — applying the truth of the Word of God in your own relationship with the Lord.

Yield Yourself to God

Place any unfulfilled dreams and desires in the hands of the Lord. If you sense a particular need today to humble yourself under God's mighty hand, that he may lift you up in due time (1 Peter 5:6), write a brief prayer expressing all that is on your heart.

Enjoy His Presence

Place today's activities, appointments, and responsibilities in the hands of the Lord.

Special Requests for Today —

One Significant Insight to Think About Today —

Rest in His Love

As you close your time with the Lord, place any anxious thoughts, conflicts, or difficult circumstances in the hands of the Lord. record a promise or verse from God's Word related to your particular need.

YIELD — ENJOY — REST

"...let us run with perseverance the race marked out for us. Let us fix our eyes on Jesus, the author and perfecter of our faith..." — Hebrews 12:1-2 NIV

SIX SECRETS TO A POWERFUL QUIET TIME ©2005

Date _____

As you close your quiet time, spend a few moments in reflection — applying the truth of the Word of God in your own relationship with the Lord.

Yield Yourself to God

Place any unfulfilled dreams and desires in the hands of the Lord. If you sense a particular need today to humble yourself under God's mighty hand, that he may lift you up in due time (1 Peter 5:6), write a brief prayer expressing all that is on your heart.

Enjoy His Presence

Place today's activities, appointments, and responsibilities in the hands of the Lord.

Special Requests for Today —

One Significant Insight to Think About Today —

Rest in His Love

As you close your time with the Lord, place any anxious thoughts, conflicts, or difficult circumstances in the hands of the Lord. record a promise or verse from God's Word related to your particular need.

YIELD — ENJOY — REST

"...let us run with perseverance the race marked out for us. Let us fix our eyes on Jesus, the author and perfecter of our faith..." — Hebrews 12:1-2 NIV

SIX SECRETS TO A POWERFUL QUIET TIME ©2005

Date _____

As you close your quiet time, spend a few moments in reflection — applying the truth of the Word of God in your own relationship with the Lord.

Yield Yourself to God

Place any unfulfilled dreams and desires in the hands of the Lord. If you sense a particular need today to humble yourself under God's mighty hand, that he may lift you up in due time (1 Peter 5:6), write a brief prayer expressing all that is on your heart.

Enjoy His Presence

Place today's activities, appointments, and responsibilities in the hands of the Lord.

Special Requests for Today —

One Significant Insight to Think About Today —

Rest in His Love

As you close your time with the Lord, place any anxious thoughts, conflicts, or difficult circumstances in the hands of the Lord. record a promise or verse from God's Word related to your particular need.

YIELD — ENJOY — REST

"...let us run with perseverance the race marked out for us. Let us fix our eyes on Jesus, the author and perfecter of our faith..." — Hebrews 12:1-2 NIV

SIX SECRETS TO A POWERFUL QUIET TIME ©2005

Date _____

As you close your quiet time, spend a few moments in reflection — applying the truth of the Word of God in your own relationship with the Lord.

Yield Yourself to God

Place any unfulfilled dreams and desires in the hands of the Lord. If you sense a particular need today to humble yourself under God's mighty hand, that he may lift you up in due time (1 Peter 5:6), write a brief prayer expressing all that is on your heart.

Enjoy His Presence

Place today's activities, appointments, and responsibilities in the hands of the Lord.

Special Requests for Today —

One Significant Insight to Think About Today —

Rest in His Love

As you close your time with the Lord, place any anxious thoughts, conflicts, or difficult circumstances in the hands of the Lord. record a promise or verse from God's Word related to your particular need.

REFERENCE STUDY

"...the grass withers and the flowers fall but the word of the Lord stands forever." — 1 Peter 1:24-25 NIV

SIX SECRETS TO A POWERFUL QUIET TIME ©2005

Verse–Topic _____ *Scripture* _____

Record observations and insights from the following references related to the selected verse or topic. Define any key words.

Key Words–Definitions

_____
Reference

_____
Reference

_____
Reference

_____
Reference

_____

Reference

_____

Reference

_____

Reference

_____

Reference

Summary–Conclusions

Application in My Life

REFERENCE STUDY

"...the grass withers and the flowers fall but the word of the Lord stands forever." — 1 Peter 1:24-25 NIV

SIX SECRETS TO A POWERFUL QUIET TIME ©2005

Verse–Topic _____ *Scripture* _____

Record observations and insights from the following references related to the selected verse or topic.
Define any key words.

Key Words–Definitions

_____

Reference

_____

Reference

_____

Reference

_____

Reference

Reference Study

_____

Reference

_____

Reference

_____

Reference

_____

Reference

Summary–Conclusions

Application in My Life

REFERENCE STUDY

PAGE ONE

"...the grass withers and the flowers fall but the word of the Lord stands forever." — 1 Peter 1:24-25 NIV

SIX SECRETS TO A POWERFUL QUIET TIME ©2005

Verse–Topic _____ *Scripture* _____

Record observations and insights from the following references related to the selected verse or topic. Define any key words.

Key Words–Definitions

_____
Reference

_____
Reference

_____
Reference

_____
Reference

_____

Reference

_____

Reference

_____

Reference

_____

Reference

Summary–Conclusions

Application in My Life

REFERENCE STUDY

PAGE ONE

"...the grass withers and the flowers fall but the word of the Lord stands forever." — 1 Peter 1:24-25 NIV

SIX SECRETS TO A POWERFUL QUIET TIME ©2005

Verse–Topic _____ *Scripture* _____

Record observations and insights from the following references related to the selected verse or topic. Define any key words.

Key Words–Definitions

_____
Reference

_____
Reference

_____
Reference

_____
Reference

Reference

Reference

Reference

Reference

Summary–Conclusions

Application in My Life

REFERENCE STUDY

PAGE ONE

"...the grass withers and the flowers fall but the word of
the Lord stands forever." — 1 Peter 1:24-25 NIV

SIX SECRETS TO A POWERFUL QUIET TIME ©2005

Verse–Topic _____ *Scripture* _____

*Record observations and insights from the following references related to the selected verse or topic.
Define any key words.*

Key Words–Definitions

_____

Reference

_____

Reference

_____

Reference

_____

Reference

_____

Reference

_____

Reference

_____

Reference

_____

Reference

Summary–Conclusions

Application in My Life

REFERENCE STUDY

PAGE ONE

"...the grass withers and the flowers fall but the word of the Lord stands forever." — 1 Peter 1:24-25 NIV

Verse–Topic _____ *Scripture* _____

Record observations and insights from the following references related to the selected verse or topic. Define any key words.

Key Words–Definitions

_____

Reference

_____

Reference

_____

Reference

_____

Reference

_____

Reference

_____

Reference

_____

Reference

_____

Reference

Summary–Conclusions

Application in My Life

REFERENCE STUDY

PAGE ONE

"...the grass withers and the flowers fall but the word of the Lord stands forever." — 1 Peter 1:24-25 NIV

SIX SECRETS TO A POWERFUL QUIET TIME ©2005

Verse–Topic _____ *Scripture* _____

Record observations and insights from the following references related to the selected verse or topic. Define any key words.

Key Words–Definitions

_____
Reference

_____
Reference

_____
Reference

_____
Reference

_____

Reference

_____

Reference

_____

Reference

_____

Reference

Summary–Conclusions

Application in My Life

REFERENCE STUDY

PAGE ONE

"...the grass withers and the flowers fall but the word of the Lord stands forever." — 1 Peter 1:24-25 NIV

SIX SECRETS TO A POWERFUL QUIET TIME ©2005

Verse–Topic _____ *Scripture* _____

Record observations and insights from the following references related to the selected verse or topic. Define any key words.

Key Words–Definitions

_____
Reference

_____
Reference

_____
Reference

_____
Reference

REFERENCE STUDY

_____

Reference

_____

Reference

_____

Reference

_____

Reference

Summary–Conclusions

Application in My Life

Reference Study

"...the grass withers and the flowers fall but the word of the Lord stands forever." — 1 Peter 1:24-25 NIV

SIX SECRETS TO A POWERFUL QUIET TIME ©2005

Verse–Topic _____ *Scripture* _____

Record observations and insights from the following references related to the selected verse or topic. Define any key words.

Key Words–Definitions

_____
Reference

_____
Reference

_____
Reference

_____
Reference

Reference

Reference

Reference

Reference

Summary–Conclusions

Application in My Life

"...the grass withers and the flowers fall but the word of the Lord stands forever." — 1 Peter 1:24-25 NIV

SIX SECRETS TO A POWERFUL QUIET TIME ©2005

Verse–Topic _____ *Scripture* _____

Record observations and insights from the following references related to the selected verse or topic. Define any key words.

Key Words–Definitions

_____

Reference

_____

Reference

_____

Reference

_____

Reference

_____

Reference

_____

Reference

_____

Reference

_____

Reference

Summary–Conclusions

Application in My Life

REFERENCE STUDY

PAGE ONE

"...the grass withers and the flowers fall but the word of the Lord stands forever." — 1 Peter 1:24-25 NIV

SIX SECRETS TO A POWERFUL QUIET TIME ©2005

Verse–Topic _____ *Scripture* _____

Record observations and insights from the following references related to the selected verse or topic. Define any key words.

Key Words–Definitions

_____

Reference

_____

Reference

_____

Reference

_____

Reference

_____

Reference

_____

Reference

_____

Reference

_____

Reference

Summary–Conclusions

Application in My Life

REFERENCE STUDY

PAGE ONE

"...the grass withers and the flowers fall but the word of
the Lord stands forever." — 1 Peter 1:24-25 NIV

SIX SECRETS TO A POWERFUL QUIET TIME ©2005

Verse–Topic _____ *Scripture* _____

*Record observations and insights from the following references related to the selected verse or topic.
Define any key words.*

Key Words–Definitions

_____

Reference

_____

Reference

_____

Reference

_____

Reference

Reference

Reference

Reference

Reference

Summary—Conclusions

Application in My Life

"...the grass withers and the flowers fall but the word of the Lord stands forever." — 1 Peter 1:24-25 NIV

SIX SECRETS TO A POWERFUL QUIET TIME ©2005

Verse–Topic _____ *Scripture* _____

Record observations and insights from the following references related to the selected verse or topic. Define any key words.

Key Words–Definitions

_____

Reference

_____

Reference

_____

Reference

_____

Reference

REFERENCE STUDY

PAGE TWO

SIX SECRETS TO A POWERFUL QUIET TIME ©2005

_____

Reference

_____

Reference

_____

Reference

_____

Reference

Summary–Conclusions

Application in My Life

REFERENCE STUDY

PAGE ONE

"...the grass withers and the flowers fall but the word of the Lord stands forever." — 1 Peter 1:24-25 NIV

Verse–Topic _____ *Scripture* _____

Record observations and insights from the following references related to the selected verse or topic. Define any key words.

Key Words–Definitions

_____

Reference

_____

Reference

_____

Reference

_____

Reference

_____

Reference

_____

Reference

_____

Reference

_____

Reference

Summary–Conclusions

Application in My Life

REFERENCE STUDY

PAGE ONE

"...the grass withers and the flowers fall but the word of
the Lord stands forever." — 1 Peter 1:24-25 NIV

Verse–Topic _____ *Scripture* _____

Record observations and insights from the following references related to the selected verse or topic.
Define any key words.

Key Words–Definitions

_____

Reference

_____

Reference

_____

Reference

_____

Reference

_____

Reference

_____

Reference

_____

Reference

_____

Reference

Summary–Conclusions

Application in My Life

"...the grass withers and the flowers fall but the word of the Lord stands forever." — 1 Peter 1:24-25 NIV

SIX SECRETS TO A POWERFUL QUIET TIME ©2005

Verse–Topic _____*Scripture* _____

Record observations and insights from the following references related to the selected verse or topic. Define any key words.

Key Words–Definitions

_____
Reference

_____
Reference

_____
Reference

_____
Reference

_____

Reference

_____

Reference

_____

Reference

_____

Reference

Summary—Conclusions

Application in My Life

REFERENCE STUDY

PAGE ONE

"...the grass withers and the flowers fall but the word of the Lord stands forever." — 1 Peter 1:24-25 NIV

SIX SECRETS TO A POWERFUL QUIET TIME ©2005

Verse–Topic _____ *Scripture* _____

Record observations and insights from the following references related to the selected verse or topic. Define any key words.

Key Words–Definitions

_____

Reference

_____

Reference

_____

Reference

_____

Reference

_____

Reference

_____

Reference

_____

Reference

_____

Reference

Summary–Conclusions

Application in My Life

REFERENCE STUDY

"...the grass withers and the flowers fall but the word of the Lord stands forever." — 1 Peter 1:24-25 NIV

SIX SECRETS TO A POWERFUL QUIET TIME ©2005

Verse–Topic _____ *Scripture* _____

Record observations and insights from the following references related to the selected verse or topic. Define any key words.

Key Words–Definitions

_____

Reference

_____

Reference

_____

Reference

_____

Reference

_____

Reference

_____

Reference

_____

Reference

_____

Reference

Summary–Conclusions

Application in My Life

REFERENCE STUDY

PAGE ONE

"...the grass withers and the flowers fall but the word of the Lord stands forever." — 1 Peter 1:24-25 NIV

SIX SECRETS TO A POWERFUL QUIET TIME ©2005

Verse–Topic _____ *Scripture* _____

Record observations and insights from the following references related to the selected verse or topic. Define any key words.

Key Words–Definitions

_____

Reference

_____

Reference

_____

Reference

_____

Reference

_____

Reference

_____

Reference

_____

Reference

_____

Reference

Summary–Conclusions

Application in My Life

Reference Study

"...the grass withers and the flowers fall but the word of
the Lord stands forever." — 1 Peter 1:24-25 NIV

SIX SECRETS TO A POWERFUL QUIET TIME ©2005

Verse–Topic _____ *Scripture* _____

Record observations and insights from the following references related to the selected verse or topic.
Define any key words.

Key Words–Definitions

_____

Reference

_____

Reference

_____

Reference

_____

Reference

_____

Reference

_____

Reference

_____

Reference

_____

Reference

Summary–Conclusions

Application in My Life

REFERENCE STUDY

PAGE ONE

"...the grass withers and the flowers fall but the word of the Lord stands forever." — 1 Peter 1:24-25 NIV

SIX SECRETS TO A POWERFUL QUIET TIME ©2005

Verse–Topic _____ *Scripture* _____

Record observations and insights from the following references related to the selected verse or topic. Define any key words.

Key Words–Definitions

_____
Reference

_____
Reference

_____
Reference

_____
Reference

Reference

Reference

Reference

Reference

Summary–Conclusions

Application in My Life

REFERENCE STUDY

PAGE ONE

"...the grass withers and the flowers fall but the word of the Lord stands forever." — 1 Peter 1:24-25 NIV

Verse–Topic _____ *Scripture* _____

Record observations and insights from the following references related to the selected verse or topic. Define any key words.

Key Words–Definitions

_____

Reference

_____

Reference

_____

Reference

_____

Reference

_____

Reference

_____

Reference

_____

Reference

_____

Reference

Summary–Conclusions

Application in My Life

REFERENCE STUDY

"...the grass withers and the flowers fall but the word of the Lord stands forever." — 1 Peter 1:24-25 NIV

SIX SECRETS TO A POWERFUL QUIET TIME ©2005

Verse–Topic _____ *Scripture* _____

Record observations and insights from the following references related to the selected verse or topic. Define any key words.

Key Words–Definitions

_____
Reference

_____
Reference

_____
Reference

_____
Reference

REFERENCE STUDY

Reference

Reference

Reference

Reference

Summary–Conclusions

Application in My Life

REFERENCE STUDY

PAGE ONE

"…the grass withers and the flowers fall but the word of the Lord stands forever." — 1 Peter 1:24-25 NIV

SIX SECRETS TO A POWERFUL QUIET TIME ©2005

Verse–Topic _____ *Scripture* _____

Record observations and insights from the following references related to the selected verse or topic. Define any key words.

Key Words–Definitions

_____
Reference

_____
Reference

_____
Reference

_____
Reference

_____

Reference

_____

Reference

_____

Reference

_____

Reference

Summary–Conclusions

Application in My Life

REFERENCE STUDY

PAGE ONE

"...the grass withers and the flowers fall but the word of the Lord stands forever." — 1 Peter 1:24-25 NIV

SIX SECRETS TO A POWERFUL QUIET TIME ©2005

Verse–Topic _____ *Scripture* _____

Record observations and insights from the following references related to the selected verse or topic.
Define any key words.

Key Words–Definitions

_____

Reference

_____

Reference

_____

Reference

_____

Reference

_____

Reference

_____

Reference

_____

Reference

_____

Reference

Summary–Conclusions

Application in My Life

REFERENCE STUDY

"...the grass withers and the flowers fall but the word of the Lord stands forever." — 1 Peter 1:24-25 NIV

SIX SECRETS TO A POWERFUL QUIET TIME ©2005

Verse–Topic _____ *Scripture* _____

Record observations and insights from the following references related to the selected verse or topic. Define any key words.

Key Words–Definitions

_____

Reference

_____

Reference

_____

Reference

_____

Reference

_____

Reference

_____

Reference

_____

Reference

_____

Reference

Summary–Conclusions

Application in My Life

REFERENCE STUDY

"...the grass withers and the flowers fall but the word of the Lord stands forever." — 1 Peter 1:24-25 NIV

SIX SECRETS TO A POWERFUL QUIET TIME ©2005

Verse–Topic _____ *Scripture* _____

Record observations and insights from the following references related to the selected verse or topic. Define any key words.

Key Words–Definitions

_____

Reference

_____

Reference

_____

Reference

_____

Reference

_____

Reference

_____

Reference

_____

Reference

_____

Reference

Summary–Conclusions

Application in My Life

REFERENCE STUDY

PAGE ONE

"...the grass withers and the flowers fall but the word of the Lord stands forever." — 1 Peter 1:24-25 NIV

SIX SECRETS TO A POWERFUL QUIET TIME ©2005

Verse–Topic _____ *Scripture* _____

Record observations and insights from the following references related to the selected verse or topic. Define any key words.

Key Words–Definitions

_____
Reference

_____
Reference

_____
Reference

_____
Reference

_____

Reference

_____

Reference

_____

Reference

_____

Reference

Summary–Conclusions

Application in My Life

REFERENCE STUDY

PAGE ONE

"...the grass withers and the flowers fall but the word of the Lord stands forever." — 1 Peter 1:24-25 NIV

Verse–Topic _____ *Scripture* _____

Record observations and insights from the following references related to the selected verse or topic. Define any key words.

Key Words–Definitions

_____
Reference

_____
Reference

_____
Reference

_____
Reference

Reference

Reference

Reference

Reference

Summary–Conclusions

Application in My Life

REFERENCE STUDY

"...the grass withers and the flowers fall but the word of the Lord stands forever." — 1 Peter 1:24-25 NIV

SIX SECRETS TO A POWERFUL QUIET TIME ©2005

Verse–Topic _____ *Scripture* _____

Record observations and insights from the following references related to the selected verse or topic. Define any key words.

Key Words–Definitions

_____
Reference

_____
Reference

_____
Reference

_____
Reference

Reference

Reference

Reference

Reference

Summary–Conclusions

Application in My Life

NOTES

"Be diligent to present yourself approved to God as a workman who does not need to be ashamed, handling accurately the word of truth." — 2 Timothy 2:15 NASB

SIX SECRETS TO A POWERFUL QUIET TIME ©2005

Date _____ Subject–Scripture _____

Title _____ Author–Speaker _____

Notes

Application In My Life

NOTES

"Be diligent to present yourself approved to God as a
workman who does not need to be ashamed, handling
accurately the word of truth." — 2 Timothy 2:15 NASB

SIX SECRETS TO A POWERFUL QUIET TIME ©2005

Date _____ Subject–Scripture _____

Title _____ Author–Speaker _____

Notes

Application In My Life

NOTES

"Be diligent to present yourself approved to God as a workman who does not need to be ashamed, handling accurately the word of truth." — 2 Timothy 2:15 NASB

SIX SECRETS TO A POWERFUL QUIET TIME ©2005

Date _____ Subject–Scripture _____

Title _____ Author–Speaker _____

Notes

Application In My Life

NOTES

"Be diligent to present yourself approved to God as a workman who does not need to be ashamed, handling accurately the word of truth." — 2 Timothy 2:15 NASB

SIX SECRETS TO A POWERFUL QUIET TIME ©2005

Date _____ Subject–Scripture _____

Title _____ Author–Speaker _____

Notes

Application In My Life

Date _____ Subject–Scripture _____

Title _____ Author–Speaker _____

Notes

Application In My Life

NOTES

"Be diligent to present yourself approved to God as a workman who does not need to be ashamed, handling accurately the word of truth." — 2 Timothy 2:15 NASB

SIX SECRETS TO A POWERFUL QUIET TIME ©2005

Date _____ *Subject–Scripture* _____

Title _____ *Author–Speaker* _____

Notes

Application In My Life

NOTES

"Be diligent to present yourself approved to God as a workman who does not need to be ashamed, handling accurately the word of truth." — 2 Timothy 2:15 NASB

SIX SECRETS TO A POWERFUL QUIET TIME ©2005

Date _____ Subject–Scripture _____

Title _____ Author–Speaker _____

Notes

Application In My Life

NOTES

"Be diligent to present yourself approved to God as a workman who does not need to be ashamed, handling accurately the word of truth." — 2 Timothy 2:15 NASB

SIX SECRETS TO A POWERFUL QUIET TIME ©2005

Date _____ Subject–Scripture _____

Title _____ Author–Speaker _____

Notes

Application In My Life

NOTES

"Be diligent to present yourself approved to God as a workman who does not need to be ashamed, handling accurately the word of truth." — 2 Timothy 2:15 NASB

Date _____ Subject–Scripture _____

Title _____ Author–Speaker _____

Notes

Application In My Life

NOTES

"Be diligent to present yourself approved to God as a workman who does not need to be ashamed, handling accurately the word of truth." — 2 Timothy 2:15 NASB

SIX SECRETS TO A POWERFUL QUIET TIME ©2005

Date _____ Subject–Scripture _____

Title _____ Author–Speaker _____

Notes

Application In My Life

NOTES

"Be diligent to present yourself approved to God as a workman who does not need to be ashamed, handling accurately the word of truth." — 2 Timothy 2:15 NASB

SIX SECRETS TO A POWERFUL QUIET TIME ©2005

Date _____ Subject–Scripture _____

Title _____ Author–Speaker _____

Notes

Application In My Life

"Be diligent to present yourself approved to God as a workman who does not need to be ashamed, handling accurately the word of truth." — 2 Timothy 2:15 NASB

SIX SECRETS TO A POWERFUL QUIET TIME ©2005

Date _____ Subject–Scripture _____

Title _____ Author–Speaker _____

Notes

Application In My Life

NOTES

"Be diligent to present yourself approved to God as a workman who does not need to be ashamed, handling accurately the word of truth." — 2 Timothy 2:15 NASB

SIX SECRETS TO A POWERFUL QUIET TIME ©2005

Date _____ Subject–Scripture _____

Title _____ Author–Speaker _____

Notes

Application In My Life

NOTES

"Be diligent to present yourself approved to God as a workman who does not need to be ashamed, handling accurately the word of truth." — 2 Timothy 2:15 NASB

SIX SECRETS TO A POWERFUL QUIET TIME ©2005

Date _____ Subject–Scripture _____

Title _____ Author–Speaker _____

Notes

Application In My Life

NOTES

"Be diligent to present yourself approved to God as a workman who does not need to be ashamed, handling accurately the word of truth." — 2 Timothy 2:15 NASB

SIX SECRETS TO A POWERFUL QUIET TIME ©2005

Date _____ Subject–Scripture _____

Title _____ Author–Speaker _____

Notes

Application In My Life

NOTES

"Be diligent to present yourself approved to God as a workman who does not need to be ashamed, handling accurately the word of truth." — 2 Timothy 2:15 NASB

SIX SECRETS TO A POWERFUL QUIET TIME ©2005

Date _____ Subject–Scripture _____

Title _____ Author–Speaker _____

Notes

Application In My Life

NOTES

"Be diligent to present yourself approved to God as a workman who does not need to be ashamed, handling accurately the word of truth." — 2 Timothy 2:15 NASB

SIX SECRETS TO A POWERFUL QUIET TIME ©2005

Date _____ Subject–Scripture _____

Title _____ Author–Speaker _____

Notes

Application In My Life

NOTES

"Be diligent to present yourself approved to God as a workman who does not need to be ashamed, handling accurately the word of truth." — 2 Timothy 2:15 NASB

Date _____ Subject–Scripture _____

Title _____ Author–Speaker _____

Notes

Application In My Life

NOTES

"Be diligent to present yourself approved to God as a workman who does not need to be ashamed, handling accurately the word of truth." — 2 Timothy 2:15 NASB

SIX SECRETS TO A POWERFUL QUIET TIME ©2005

Date _____ Subject–Scripture _____

Title _____ Author–Speaker _____

Notes

Application In My Life

"Be diligent to present yourself approved to God as a workman who does not need to be ashamed, handling accurately the word of truth." — 2 Timothy 2:15 NASB

SIX SECRETS TO A POWERFUL QUIET TIME ©2005

Date _____ Subject–Scripture _____

Title _____ Author–Speaker _____

Notes

Application In My Life

NOTES

"Be diligent to present yourself approved to God as a workman who does not need to be ashamed, handling accurately the word of truth." — 2 Timothy 2:15 NASB

Date _____ Subject–Scripture _____

Title _____ Author–Speaker _____

Notes

Application In My Life

NOTES

"Be diligent to present yourself approved to God as a workman who does not need to be ashamed, handling accurately the word of truth." — 2 Timothy 2:15 NASB

SIX SECRETS TO A POWERFUL QUIET TIME ©2005

Date _____ Subject–Scripture _____

Title _____ Author–Speaker _____

Notes

Application In My Life

NOTES

"Be diligent to present yourself approved to God as a workman who does not need to be ashamed, handling accurately the word of truth." — 2 Timothy 2:15 NASB

Date _____ Subject–Scripture _____

Title _____ Author–Speaker _____

Notes

Application In My Life

NOTES

"Be diligent to present yourself approved to God as a workman who does not need to be ashamed, handling accurately the word of truth." — 2 Timothy 2:15 NASB

SIX SECRETS TO A POWERFUL QUIET TIME ©2005

Date _____ Subject–Scripture _____

Title _____ Author–Speaker _____

Notes

Application In My Life

NOTES

"Be diligent to present yourself approved to God as a workman who does not need to be ashamed, handling accurately the word of truth." — 2 Timothy 2:15 NASB

SIX SECRETS TO A POWERFUL QUIET TIME ©2005

Date _____ Subject–Scripture _____

Title _____ Author–Speaker _____

Notes

Application In My Life

NOTES

"Be diligent to present yourself approved to God as a workman who does not need to be ashamed, handling accurately the word of truth." — 2 Timothy 2:15 NASB

SIX SECRETS TO A POWERFUL QUIET TIME ©2005

Date _____ Subject–Scripture _____

Title _____ Author–Speaker _____

Notes

Application In My Life

NOTES

"Be diligent to present yourself approved to God as a workman who does not need to be ashamed, handling accurately the word of truth." — 2 Timothy 2:15 NASB

SIX SECRETS TO A POWERFUL QUIET TIME ©2005

Date _____ Subject–Scripture _____

Title _____ Author–Speaker _____

Notes

Application In My Life

NOTES

"Be diligent to present yourself approved to God as a workman who does not need to be ashamed, handling accurately the word of truth." — 2 Timothy 2:15 NASB

SIX SECRETS TO A POWERFUL QUIET TIME ©2005

Date _____ Subject–Scripture _____

Title _____ Author–Speaker _____

Notes

Application In My Life

NOTES

"Be diligent to present yourself approved to God as a workman who does not need to be ashamed, handling accurately the word of truth." — 2 Timothy 2:15 NASB

SIX SECRETS TO A POWERFUL QUIET TIME ©2005

Date _____ Subject–Scripture _____

Title _____ Author–Speaker _____

Notes

Application In My Life

NOTES

"Be diligent to present yourself approved to God as a workman who does not need to be ashamed, handling accurately the word of truth." — 2 Timothy 2:15 NASB

Date _____ Subject–Scripture _____

Title _____ Author–Speaker _____

Notes

Application In My Life

NOTES

"Be diligent to present yourself approved to God as a workman who does not need to be ashamed, handling accurately the word of truth." — 2 Timothy 2:15 NASB

Date _____ *Subject–Scripture* _____

Title _____ *Author–Speaker* _____

Notes

Application In My Life

NOTES

"Be diligent to present yourself approved to God as a workman who does not need to be ashamed, handling accurately the word of truth." — 2 Timothy 2:15 NASB

Date _____ *Subject–Scripture* _____

Title _____ *Author–Speaker* _____

Notes

Application In My Life

NOTES

"Be diligent to present yourself approved to God as a workman who does not need to be ashamed, handling accurately the word of truth." — 2 Timothy 2:15 NASB

SIX SECRETS TO A POWERFUL QUIET TIME ©2005

Date _____ Subject–Scripture _____

Title _____ Author–Speaker _____

Notes

Application In My Life

NOTES

"Be diligent to present yourself approved to God as a workman who does not need to be ashamed, handling accurately the word of truth." — 2 Timothy 2:15 NASB

SIX SECRETS TO A POWERFUL QUIET TIME ©2005

Date _____ Subject–Scripture _____

Title _____ Author–Speaker _____

Notes

Application In My Life

NOTES

"Be diligent to present yourself approved to God as a workman who does not need to be ashamed, handling accurately the word of truth." — 2 Timothy 2:15 NASB

SIX SECRETS TO A POWERFUL QUIET TIME ©2005

Date _____ Subject–Scripture _____

Title _____ Author–Speaker _____

Notes

Application In My Life

NOTES

"Be diligent to present yourself approved to God as a workman who does not need to be ashamed, handling accurately the word of truth." — 2 Timothy 2:15 NASB

SIX SECRETS TO A POWERFUL QUIET TIME ©2005

Date _____ Subject–Scripture _____

Title _____ Author–Speaker _____

Notes

Application In My Life

NOTES

"Be diligent to present yourself approved to God as a workman who does not need to be ashamed, handling accurately the word of truth." — 2 Timothy 2:15 NASB

SIX SECRETS TO A POWERFUL QUIET TIME ©2005

Date _____ Subject–Scripture _____

Title _____ Author–Speaker _____

Notes

Application In My Life

NOTES

"Be diligent to present yourself approved to God as a
workman who does not need to be ashamed, handling
accurately the word of truth." — 2 Timothy 2:15 NASB

SIX SECRETS TO A POWERFUL QUIET TIME ©2005

Date _____ Subject–Scripture _____

Title _____ Author–Speaker _____

Notes

Application In My Life

NOTES

"Be diligent to present yourself approved to God as a workman who does not need to be ashamed, handling accurately the word of truth." — 2 Timothy 2:15 NASB

SIX SECRETS TO A POWERFUL QUIET TIME ©2005

Date _____ Subject–Scripture _____

Title _____ Author–Speaker _____

Notes

Application In My Life

"Be diligent to present yourself approved to God as a workman who does not need to be ashamed, handling accurately the word of truth." — 2 Timothy 2:15 NASB

SIX SECRETS TO A POWERFUL QUIET TIME ©2005

Date _____ Subject–Scripture _____

Title _____ Author–Speaker _____

Notes

Application In My Life

NOTES

"Be diligent to present yourself approved to God as a workman who does not need to be ashamed, handling accurately the word of truth." — 2 Timothy 2:15 NASB

Date _____ Subject–Scripture _____

Title _____ Author–Speaker _____

Notes

Application In My Life

NOTES

"Be diligent to present yourself approved to God as a workman who does not need to be ashamed, handling accurately the word of truth." — 2 Timothy 2:15 NASB

SIX SECRETS TO A POWERFUL QUIET TIME ©2005

Date _____ Subject–Scripture _____

Title _____ Author–Speaker _____

Notes

Application In My Life

NOTES

"Be diligent to present yourself approved to God as a workman who does not need to be ashamed, handling accurately the word of truth." — 2 Timothy 2:15 NASB

Date _____ Subject–Scripture _____

Title _____ Author–Speaker _____

Notes

Application In My Life

NOTES

"Be diligent to present yourself approved to God as a workman who does not need to be ashamed, handling accurately the word of truth." — 2 Timothy 2:15 NASB

SIX SECRETS TO A POWERFUL QUIET TIME ©2005

Date _____ Subject–Scripture _____

Title _____ Author–Speaker _____

Notes

Application In My Life

NOTES

"Be diligent to present yourself approved to God as a workman who does not need to be ashamed, handling accurately the word of truth." — 2 Timothy 2:15 NASB

SIX SECRETS TO A POWERFUL QUIET TIME ©2005

Date _____ Subject–Scripture _____

Title _____ Author–Speaker _____

Notes

Application In My Life

NOTES

"Be diligent to present yourself approved to God as a workman who does not need to be ashamed, handling accurately the word of truth." — 2 Timothy 2:15 NASB

SIX SECRETS TO A POWERFUL QUIET TIME ©2005

Date _____ Subject–Scripture _____

Title _____ Author–Speaker _____

Notes

Application In My Life

NOTES

"Be diligent to present yourself approved to God as a workman who does not need to be ashamed, handling accurately the word of truth." — 2 Timothy 2:15 NASB

SIX SECRETS TO A POWERFUL QUIET TIME ©2005

Date _____ Subject–Scripture _____

Title _____ Author–Speaker _____

Notes

Application In My Life

NOTES

"Be diligent to present yourself approved to God as a
workman who does not need to be ashamed, handling
accurately the word of truth." — 2 Timothy 2:15 NASB

SIX SECRETS TO A POWERFUL QUIET TIME ©2005

Date _____ Subject–Scripture _____

Title _____ Author–Speaker _____

Notes

Application In My Life

NOTES

"Be diligent to present yourself approved to God as a workman who does not need to be ashamed, handling accurately the word of truth." — 2 Timothy 2:15 NASB

SIX SECRETS TO A POWERFUL QUIET TIME ©2005

Date _____ Subject–Scripture _____

Title _____ Author–Speaker _____

Notes

Application In My Life

NOTES

"Be diligent to present yourself approved to God as a workman who does not need to be ashamed, handling accurately the word of truth." — 2 Timothy 2:15 NASB

SIX SECRETS TO A POWERFUL QUIET TIME ©2005

Date _____ *Subject–Scripture* _____

Title _____ *Author–Speaker* _____

Notes

Application In My Life

NOTES

"Be diligent to present yourself approved to God as a workman who does not need to be ashamed, handling accurately the word of truth." — 2 Timothy 2:15 NASB

SIX SECRETS TO A POWERFUL QUIET TIME ©2005

Date _____ Subject–Scripture _____

Title _____ Author–Speaker _____

Notes

Application In My Life

433

NOTES

"Be diligent to present yourself approved to God as a workman who does not need to be ashamed, handling accurately the word of truth." — 2 Timothy 2:15 NASB

Date _____ Subject–Scripture _____

Title _____ Author–Speaker _____

Notes

Application In My Life

NOTES

"Be diligent to present yourself approved to God as a workman who does not need to be ashamed, handling accurately the word of truth." — 2 Timothy 2:15 NASB

SIX SECRETS TO A POWERFUL QUIET TIME ©2005

Date _____ Subject–Scripture _____

Title _____ Author–Speaker _____

Notes

Application In My Life

NOTES

"Be diligent to present yourself approved to God as a workman who does not need to be ashamed, handling accurately the word of truth." — 2 Timothy 2:15 NASB

SIX SECRETS TO A POWERFUL QUIET TIME ©2005

Date _____ Subject–Scripture _____

Title _____ Author–Speaker _____

Notes

Application In My Life

NOTES

"Be diligent to present yourself approved to God as a workman who does not need to be ashamed, handling accurately the word of truth." — 2 Timothy 2:15 NASB

SIX SECRETS TO A POWERFUL QUIET TIME ©2005

Date _____ Subject–Scripture _____

Title _____ Author–Speaker _____

Notes

Application In My Life

NOTES

"Be diligent to present yourself approved to God as a workman who does not need to be ashamed, handling accurately the word of truth." — 2 Timothy 2:15 NASB

SIX SECRETS TO A POWERFUL QUIET TIME ©2005

Date _____ *Subject–Scripture* _____

Title _____ *Author–Speaker* _____

Notes

Application In My Life

NOTES

"Be diligent to present yourself approved to God as a workman who does not need to be ashamed, handling accurately the word of truth." — 2 Timothy 2:15 NASB

SIX SECRETS TO A POWERFUL QUIET TIME ©2005

Date _____ *Subject–Scripture* _____

Title _____ *Author–Speaker* _____

Notes

Application In My Life

NOTES

"Be diligent to present yourself approved to God as a workman who does not need to be ashamed, handling accurately the word of truth." — 2 Timothy 2:15 NASB

SIX SECRETS TO A POWERFUL QUIET TIME ©2005

Date _____ Subject–Scripture _____

Title _____ Author–Speaker _____

Notes

Application In My Life

NOTES

"Be diligent to present yourself approved to God as a workman who does not need to be ashamed, handling accurately the word of truth." — 2 Timothy 2:15 NASB

SIX SECRETS TO A POWERFUL QUIET TIME ©2005

Date _____ Subject–Scripture _____

Title _____ Author–Speaker _____

Notes

Application In My Life

"Be diligent to present yourself approved to God as a workman who does not need to be ashamed, handling accurately the word of truth." — 2 Timothy 2:15 NASB

SIX SECRETS TO A POWERFUL QUIET TIME ©2005

Date _____ Subject–Scripture _____

Title _____ Author–Speaker _____

Notes

Application In My Life

APPENDIX

About Catherine Martin
Notes
Quiet Time Ministries Resources

ABOUT THE AUTHOR

Catherine Martin is a summa cum laude graduate of Bethel Theological Seminary with a Master of Arts degree in Theological Studies. She is founder and president of Quiet Time Ministries, director of women's ministries at Southwest Community Church in Indian Wells, California, and adjunct faculty member of Biola University. She is the author of *Six Secrets to a Powerful Quiet Time, Knowing and Loving the Bible, Walking with the God Who Cares, Set my Heart on Fire, Trusting in the Names of God, Passionate Prayer, Quiet Time Moments for Women,* and *Drawing Strength from the Names of God* published by Harvest House Publishers, and *Pilgrimage of the Heart, Revive My Heart!* and *A Heart That Dances,* published by NavPress. She has also written *The Quiet Time Notebook, A Heart on Fire, A Heart to See Forever,* and *A Heart That Hopes in God,* published by Quiet Time Ministries. She is senior editor for *Enriching Your Quiet Time* quarterly magazine. As a popular speaker at retreats and conferences, Catherine challenges others to seek God and love Him with all of their heart, soul, mind, and strength. For more information about Catherine, visit www.quiettime.org.

ABOUT QUIET TIME MINISTRIES

Quiet Time Ministries is a nonprofit religious organization under Section 501(c)(3) of the Internal Revenue Code. Cash donations are tax deductible as charitable contributions. We count on prayerful donors like you, partners with Quiet Time Ministries pursuing our goals of the furtherance of the Gospel of Jesus Christ and teaching devotion to God and His Word. Visit us online at www.quiettime.org to view special funding opportunities and current ministry projects. Your prayerful donations bring countless project to life!

Quiet Time Ministries | P.O. Box 14007 | Palm Desert, California 92255
1.800.925.6458 | catherine@quiettime.org | www.quiettime.org

NOTES

CHAPTER 1

1. Used by permission from *A Place Apart* by Basil M. Pennington, copyright © 1998 Liguori Publications, Liguori, MO 63057, 1-800-325-9521..

2. Henri Nouwen, *The Way of the Heart* (New York: Ballantine Books, 1981), p. 17.

3. A.A. Bonar and R. McCheyne, Memoirs and Remains of Robert Murray McCheyne (Carlisle, PA: Banner of truth Trust, 1996).

4. Henri Nouwen, "Moving from Solitude to Community to Ministry," *Leadership Journal*, Sping 1995, p. 81.

CHAPTER 7

1. Caatherine Martin, *A Woman's Walk in Grace* (Eugene, OR: Harvest House Publishers, 2010), p. 24.

CHAPTER 8

1. Quiet time adapted from Pilgrimage of the Heart, Catherine Martin (Colorado Springs, CO: NavPress 2003) pp. 133-136.

CATHERINE MARTIN

Author of *The Quiet Time Notebook*

THE QUIET TIME JOURNAL

Pouring Out Your Soul To The Lord

CATHERINE MARTIN

Author of *Knowing & Loving The Bible*

THE DEVOTIONAL BIBLE STUDY NOTEBOOK

Premium Quiet Time Devotional Studies

CATHERINE MARTIN

Author of *Passionate Prayer*

THE
PASSIONATE
PRAYER
NOTEBOOK

The Passionate Prayer Growth Plan

THE PASSIONATE PRAYER NOTEBOOK

MARTIN

A 30-DAY JOURNEY

SIX SECRETS TO A POWERFUL QUIET TIME

Discovering Radical Intimacy with God

Catherine Martin

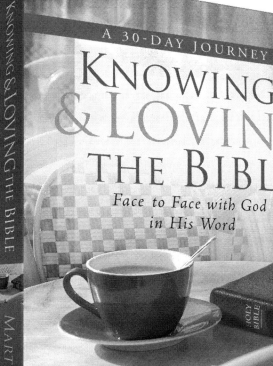

A 30-DAY JOURNEY

KNOWING & LOVING THE BIBLE

Face to Face with God in His Word

Foreword by
JOSH McDOWELL

CATHERINE MARTIN

Author of *Six Secrets to a Powerful Quiet Time*

Made in the USA
Monee, IL
22 January 2024

51736884R00249